MW01641577

Soups

Soups

GALLERY BOOKS
An Imprint of W. H. Smith Publishers Inc.
112 Madison Avenue
New York City 10016

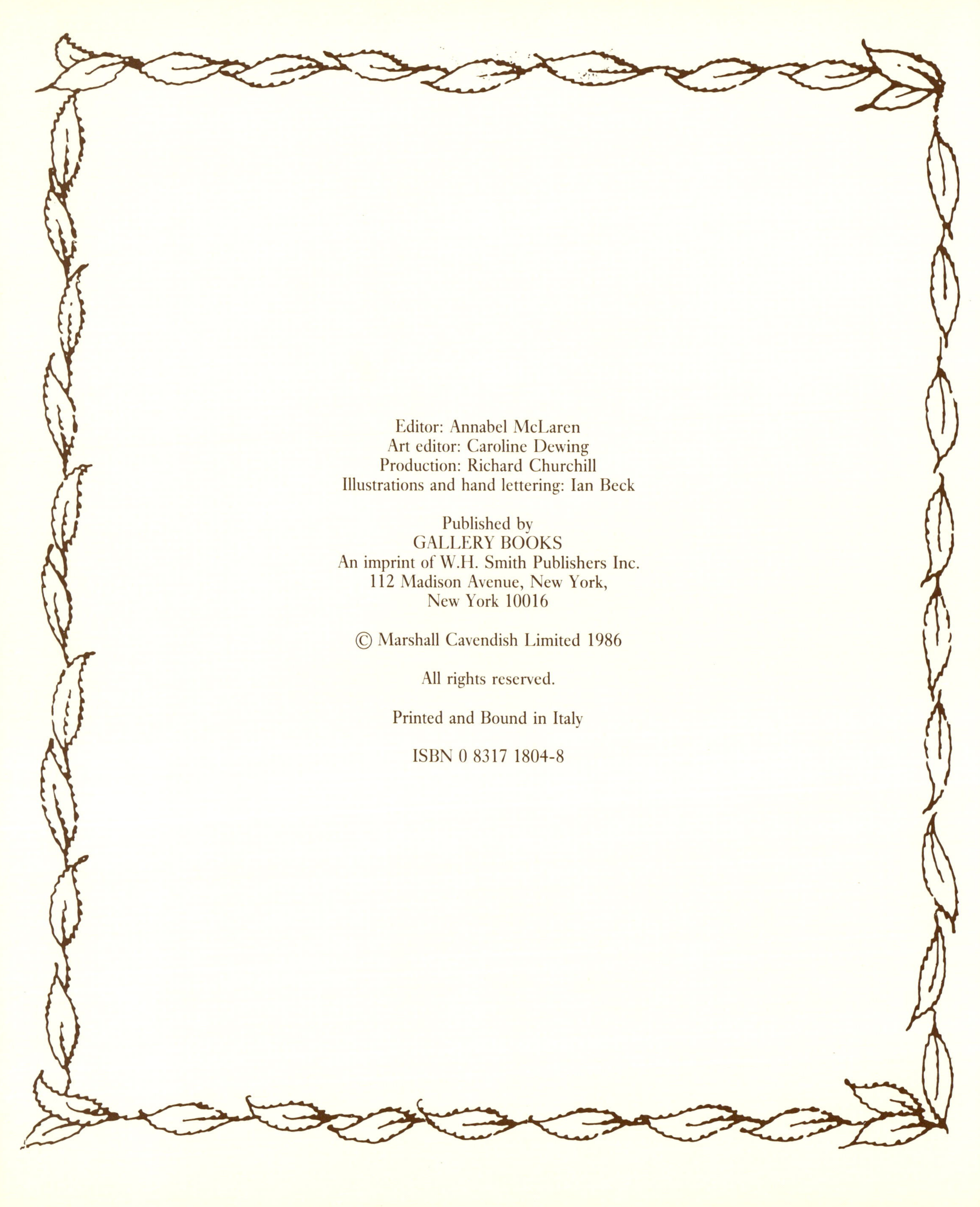

Editor: Annabel McLaren
Art editor: Caroline Dewing
Production: Richard Churchill
Illustrations and hand lettering: Ian Beck

Published by
GALLERY BOOKS
An imprint of W.H. Smith Publishers Inc.
112 Madison Avenue, New York,
New York 10016

Printed and Bound in Italy

ISBN 0 8317 1804-8

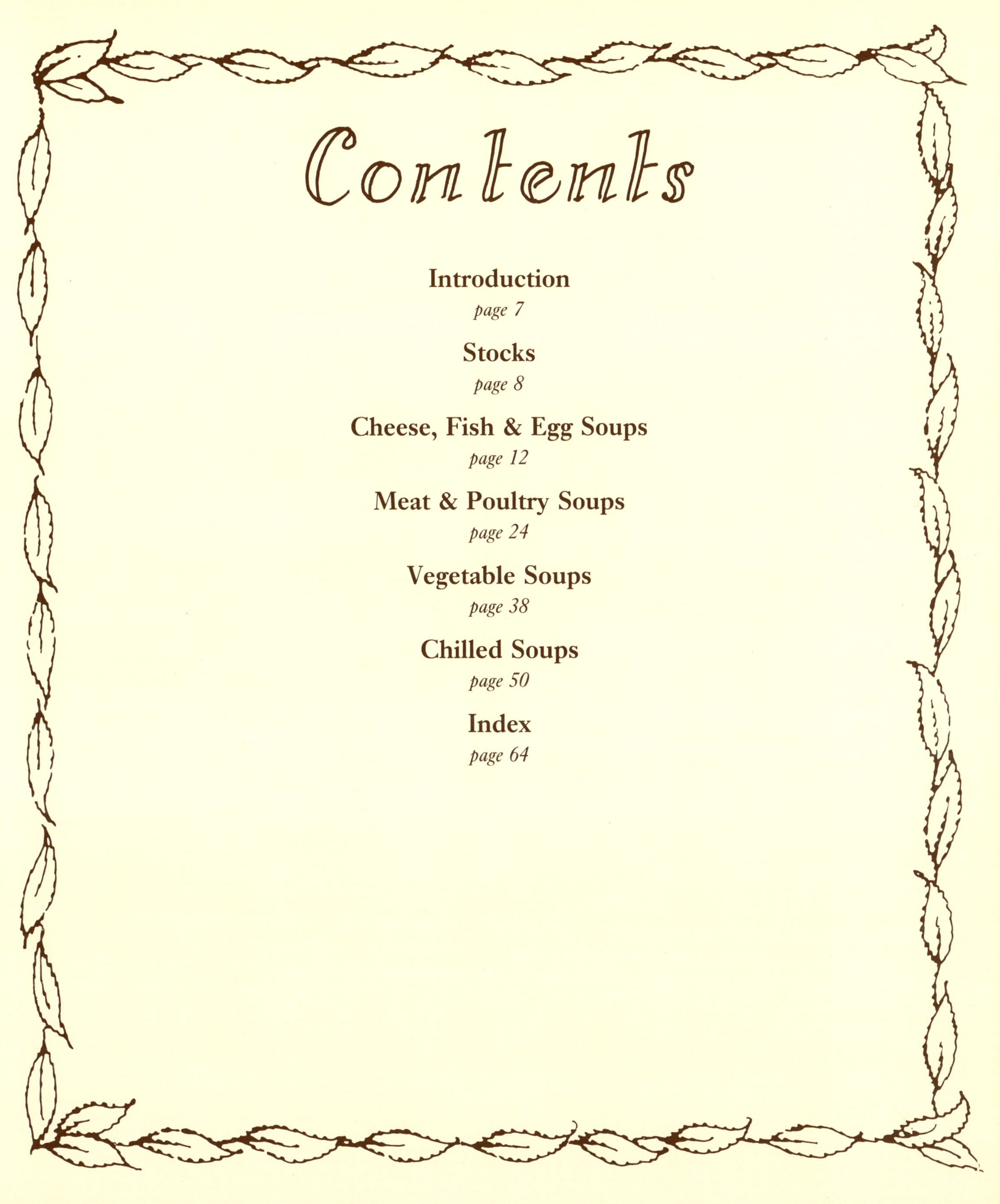

Contents

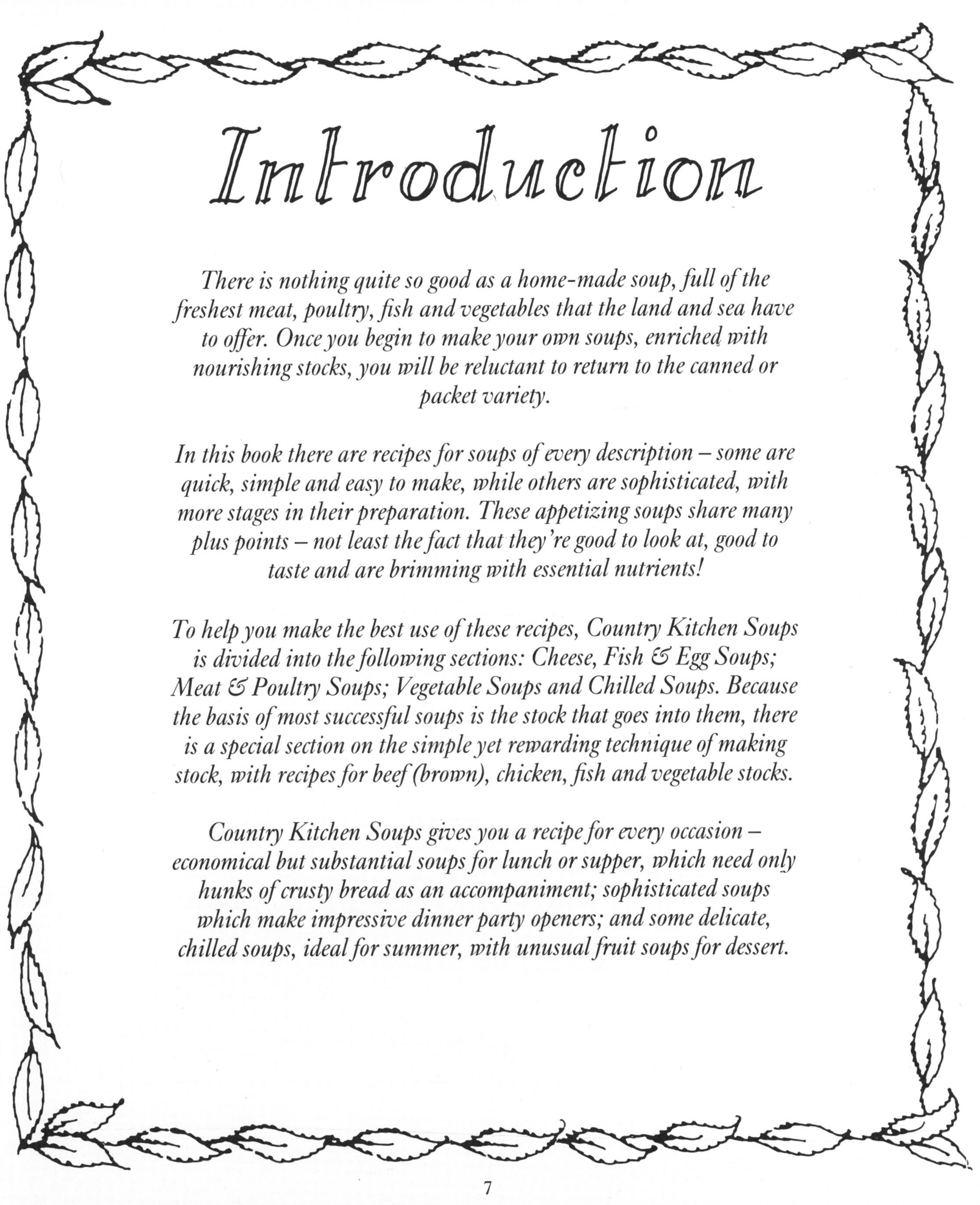

Introduction

There is nothing quite so good as a home-made soup, full of the freshest meat, poultry, fish and vegetables that the land and sea have to offer. Once you begin to make your own soups, enriched with nourishing stocks, you will be reluctant to return to the canned or packet variety.

In this book there are recipes for soups of every description – some are quick, simple and easy to make, while others are sophisticated, with more stages in their preparation. These appetizing soups share many plus points – not least the fact that they're good to look at, good to taste and are brimming with essential nutrients!

To help you make the best use of these recipes, Country Kitchen Soups is divided into the following sections: Cheese, Fish & Egg Soups; Meat & Poultry Soups; Vegetable Soups and Chilled Soups. Because the basis of most successful soups is the stock that goes into them, there is a special section on the simple yet rewarding technique of making stock, with recipes for beef (brown), chicken, fish and vegetable stocks.

Country Kitchen Soups gives you a recipe for every occasion – economical but substantial soups for lunch or supper, which need only hunks of crusty bread as an accompaniment; sophisticated soups which make impressive dinner party openers; and some delicate, chilled soups, ideal for summer, with unusual fruit soups for dessert.

Stocks

Every good soup starts with a simple yet superb stock. The recipes that follow are all easy to make and form the basis of many of the soups in the book. Make them whenever you have time to spare and, for convenience, store them in the refrigerator or freezer.
Beef stock and Chicken stock keep in the refrigerator for up to a week if boiled every day, while Fish stock, which also needs daily boiling, keeps for two days. Vegetable stock is best used freshly made, but all freeze well. Fish and Vegetable stocks keep for three months, while beef or poultry stocks keep up to six.

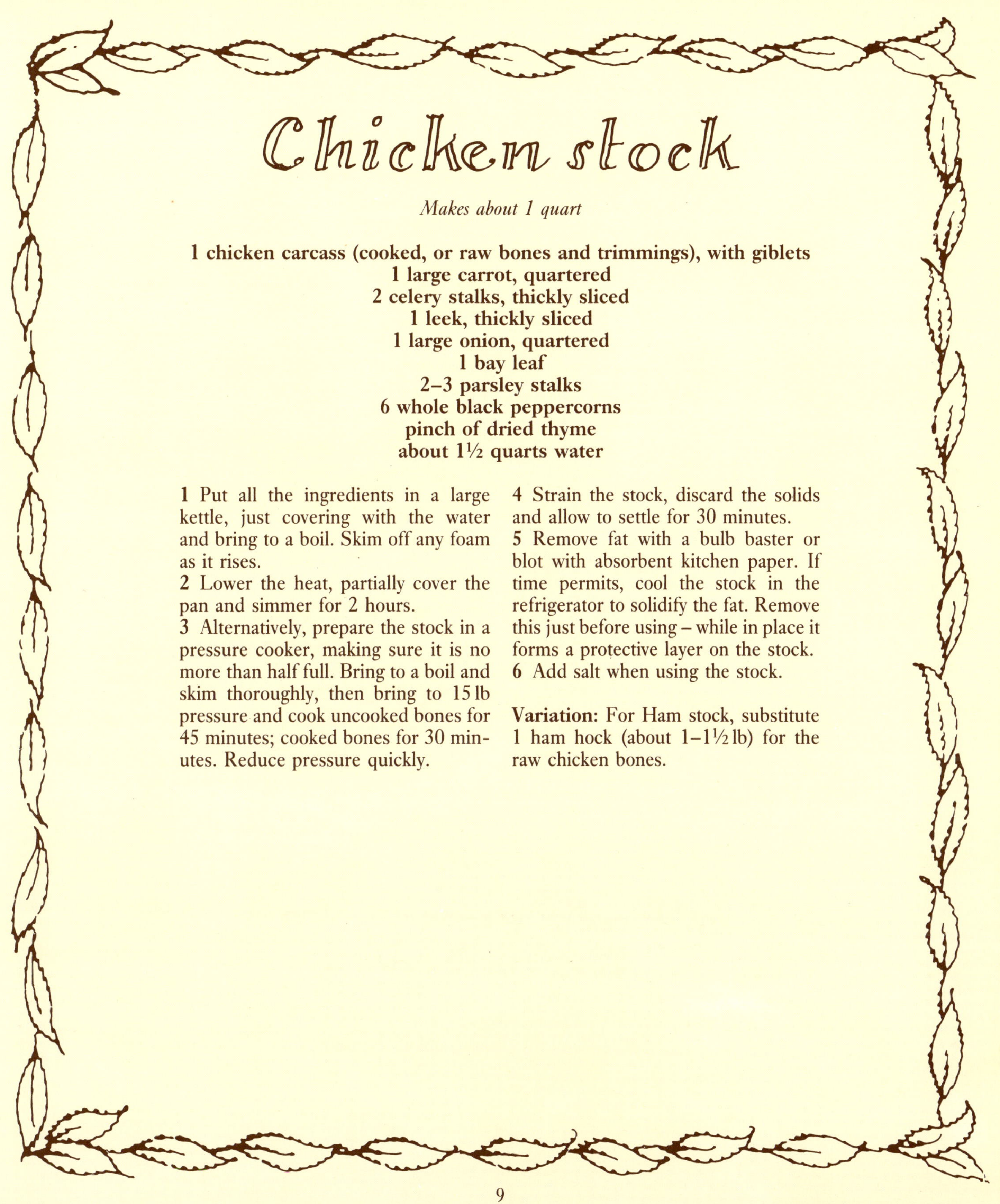

Chicken stock

Makes about 1 quart

1 chicken carcass (cooked, or raw bones and trimmings), with giblets
1 large carrot, quartered
2 celery stalks, thickly sliced
1 leek, thickly sliced
1 large onion, quartered
1 bay leaf
2–3 parsley stalks
6 whole black peppercorns
pinch of dried thyme
about 1½ quarts water

1 Put all the ingredients in a large kettle, just covering with the water and bring to a boil. Skim off any foam as it rises.
2 Lower the heat, partially cover the pan and simmer for 2 hours.
3 Alternatively, prepare the stock in a pressure cooker, making sure it is no more than half full. Bring to a boil and skim thoroughly, then bring to 15 lb pressure and cook uncooked bones for 45 minutes; cooked bones for 30 minutes. Reduce pressure quickly.
4 Strain the stock, discard the solids and allow to settle for 30 minutes.
5 Remove fat with a bulb baster or blot with absorbent kitchen paper. If time permits, cool the stock in the refrigerator to solidify the fat. Remove this just before using – while in place it forms a protective layer on the stock.
6 Add salt when using the stock.

Variation: For Ham stock, substitute 1 ham hock (about 1–1½ lb) for the raw chicken bones.

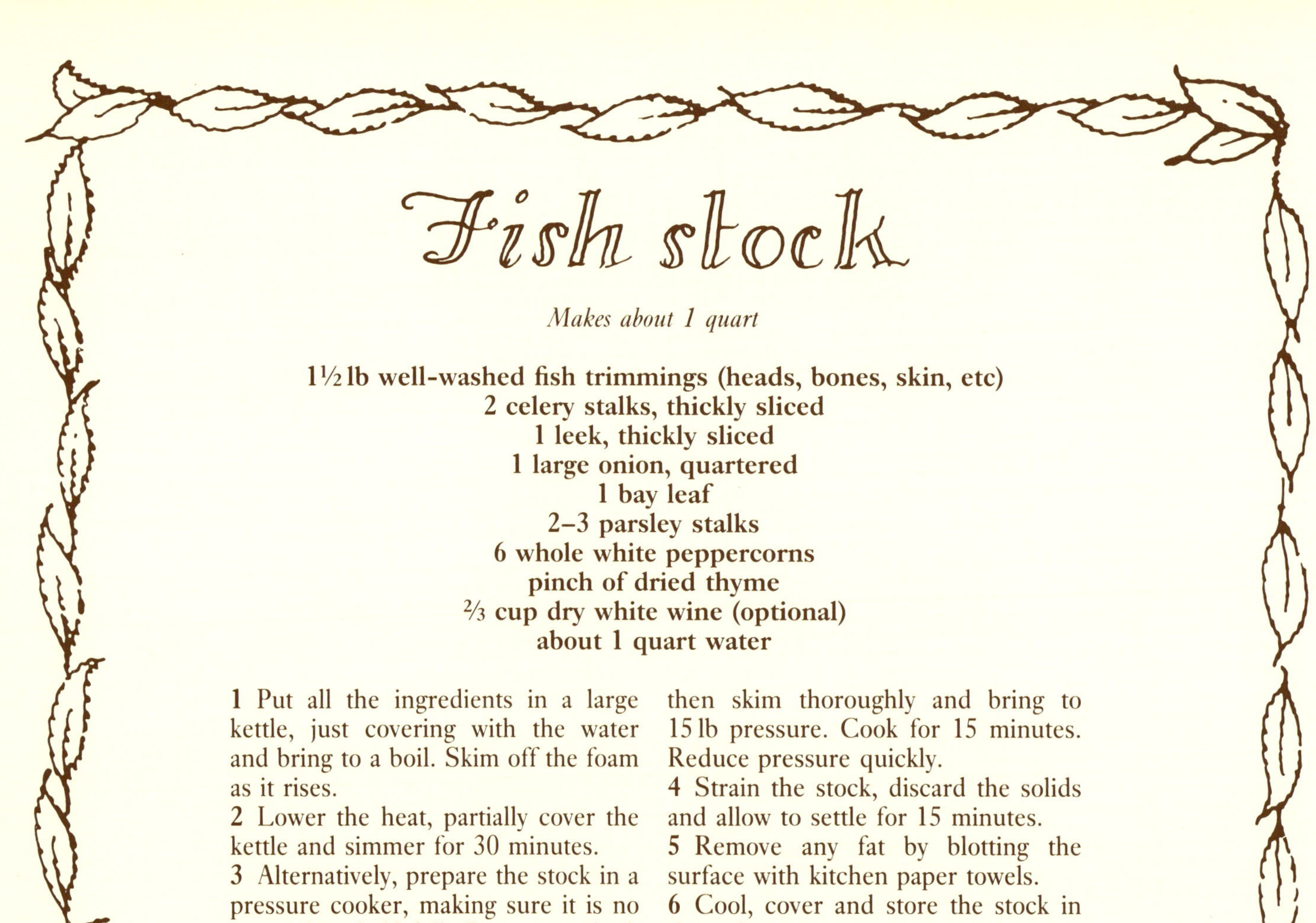

Fish stock

Makes about 1 quart

1½ lb well-washed fish trimmings (heads, bones, skin, etc)
2 celery stalks, thickly sliced
1 leek, thickly sliced
1 large onion, quartered
1 bay leaf
2–3 parsley stalks
6 whole white peppercorns
pinch of dried thyme
⅔ cup dry white wine (optional)
about 1 quart water

1 Put all the ingredients in a large kettle, just covering with the water and bring to a boil. Skim off the foam as it rises.

2 Lower the heat, partially cover the kettle and simmer for 30 minutes.

3 Alternatively, prepare the stock in a pressure cooker, making sure it is no more than half full. Bring to a boil, then skim thoroughly and bring to 15 lb pressure. Cook for 15 minutes. Reduce pressure quickly.

4 Strain the stock, discard the solids and allow to settle for 15 minutes.

5 Remove any fat by blotting the surface with kitchen paper towels.

6 Cool, cover and store the stock in the refrigerator.

Beef (brown) stock

Makes about 1 quart

2 lb raw beef marrow bones or a mixture of beef and veal
1 large carrot, quartered
3 celery stalks, thickly sliced
1 large onion, quartered, skins reserved
1 bay leaf
2–3 parsley stalks
pinch of dried thyme
about 2 quarts water

1 Preheat the oven to 425°F. Put the bones, carrot, celery and onion into a roasting pan and cook in the oven for 40 minutes, basting from time to time.
2 With a slotted spoon, transfer the bones and vegetables to a large kettle and add the remaining ingredients including the onion skins. Just cover with about 2 quarts of water and bring to a boil. Skim off any foam as it rises.
3 Lower the heat, partially cover the kettle and simmer for about 4 hours.
4 Alternatively, prepare the stock in a pressure cooker, making sure it is no more than half full. Place the roasted bones and other ingredients in a pressure cooker, bring to a boil and skim thoroughly. Then bring to 15 lb pressure and cook for 1 hour. Reduce pressure quickly.
5 To degrease, follow steps 4–6 in the recipe for Chicken stock.

Vegetable stock

Makes about 1 quart

2 tablespoons olive oil
2 cups finely chopped onions
2 large potatoes, diced
2 celery stalks, finely sliced
1 large parsnip, peeled, quartered and thinly sliced
1 turnip, peeled, quartered and thinly sliced
2 bay leaves
2 parsley stalks
4 cups water

1 Heat the oil in a large kettle, add the onions, potatoes and celery and cook over gentle heat for 10 minutes, stirring constantly until the vegetables are cooked but not colored.
2 Stir in the remaining vegetables along with the bay leaves and parsley. Add the water, bring to a boil, lower the heat and simmer gently for 1 hour.
3 Alternatively, prepare the stock in a pressure cooker, making sure it is no more than half full. Bring to a boil and skim thoroughly, then bring to 15 lb pressure and cook for 15 minutes. Reduce the pressure quickly.
4 Pour the stock through a fine strainer, pressing the vegetables against the side with a wooden spoon to extract as much flavor as possible. Take care not to let any of the vegetable mixture pass through the mesh of the strainer.
5 Cool the stock, cover and store in the refrigerator for up to three months. Add salt when using the stock if desired.

Cheese, Fish & Egg Soups

With their robust flavor and smooth texture, cheese soups may be a new taste sensation – once you've tried one, you're sure to repeat the experience! Family and friends will savor the taste of soups houed with sharp Cheddar, or made smooth with creamy blue cheese. Fish soups also feature in this chapter – from chunky chowders to simple shellfish soups, guaranteed to bring out all the flavor of the catch. Add eggs to a soup and you have a complete meal – the Italians have known this for years! Blended with the stock, poached in the cooking liquid, or combined with flour to make delicious dumplings, eggs add something special to a soup.

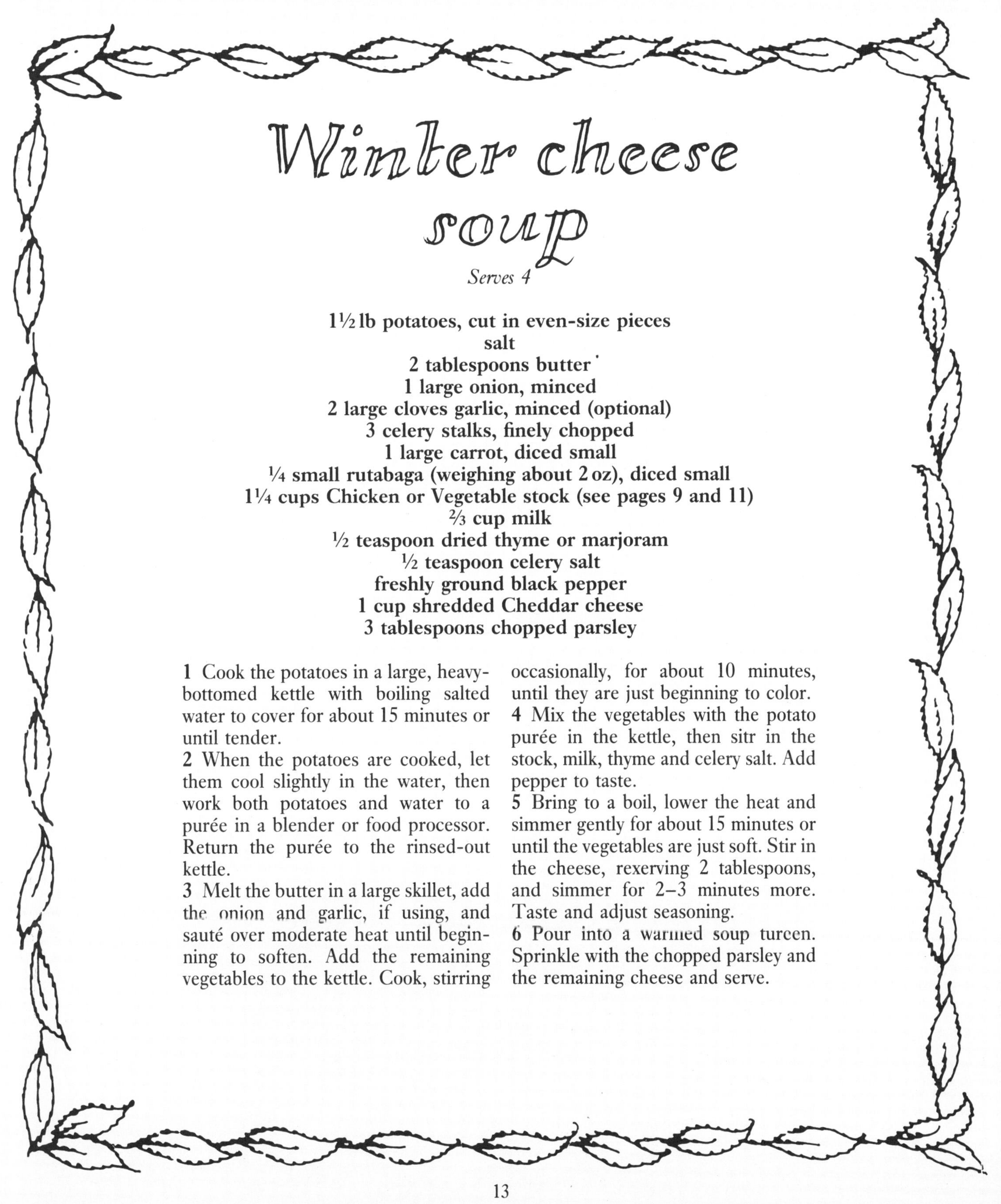

Winter cheese soup

Serves 4

1½ lb potatoes, cut in even-size pieces
salt
2 tablespoons butter
1 large onion, minced
2 large cloves garlic, minced (optional)
3 celery stalks, finely chopped
1 large carrot, diced small
¼ small rutabaga (weighing about 2 oz), diced small
1¼ cups Chicken or Vegetable stock (see pages 9 and 11)
⅔ cup milk
½ teaspoon dried thyme or marjoram
½ teaspoon celery salt
freshly ground black pepper
1 cup shredded Cheddar cheese
3 tablespoons chopped parsley

1 Cook the potatoes in a large, heavy-bottomed kettle with boiling salted water to cover for about 15 minutes or until tender.

2 When the potatoes are cooked, let them cool slightly in the water, then work both potatoes and water to a purée in a blender or food processor. Return the purée to the rinsed-out kettle.

3 Melt the butter in a large skillet, add the onion and garlic, if using, and sauté over moderate heat until beginning to soften. Add the remaining vegetables to the kettle. Cook, stirring occasionally, for about 10 minutes, until they are just beginning to color.

4 Mix the vegetables with the potato purée in the kettle, then sitr in the stock, milk, thyme and celery salt. Add pepper to taste.

5 Bring to a boil, lower the heat and simmer gently for about 15 minutes or until the vegetables are just soft. Stir in the cheese, rexerving 2 tablespoons, and simmer for 2–3 minutes more. Taste and adjust seasoning.

6 Pour into a warmed soup tureen. Sprinkle with the chopped parsley and the remaining cheese and serve.

Blue cheese & celery soup

Serves 4

3 tablespoons butter
1 head celery, finely chopped
2 large leeks, thinly sliced
3 cups Chicken stock (see page 9)
2 large egg yolks
¼ cup light cream
¼ lb mild blue cheese, trimmed of rind
salt and freshly ground black pepper

1 Melt the butter in a large, heavy-bottomed saucepan. Add the celery and leeks, cover and cook gently, stirring occasionally, for about 10 minutes, until the vegetables are soft.

2 Add the stock and bring to a boil. Lower the heat and simmer, uncovered, for about 20 minutes, until vegetables are tender. Cool slightly, then work to a purée in a blender or food processor.

3 Return the soup to the rinsed-out pan and reheat very gently, without bringing to a boil.

4 Meanwhile, beat the egg yolks and cream together until they are smoothly blended. In a separate bowl, mash the cheese to a rough paste with a fork, then gradually work in the egg and cream mixture.

5 Stir a spoonful of the hot soup into the cheese mixture, then pour the mixture back into the pan, stirring constantly until the soup has thickened slightly. Season with salt and freshly ground black pepper to taste, then serve the soup at once, in warmed individual bowls.

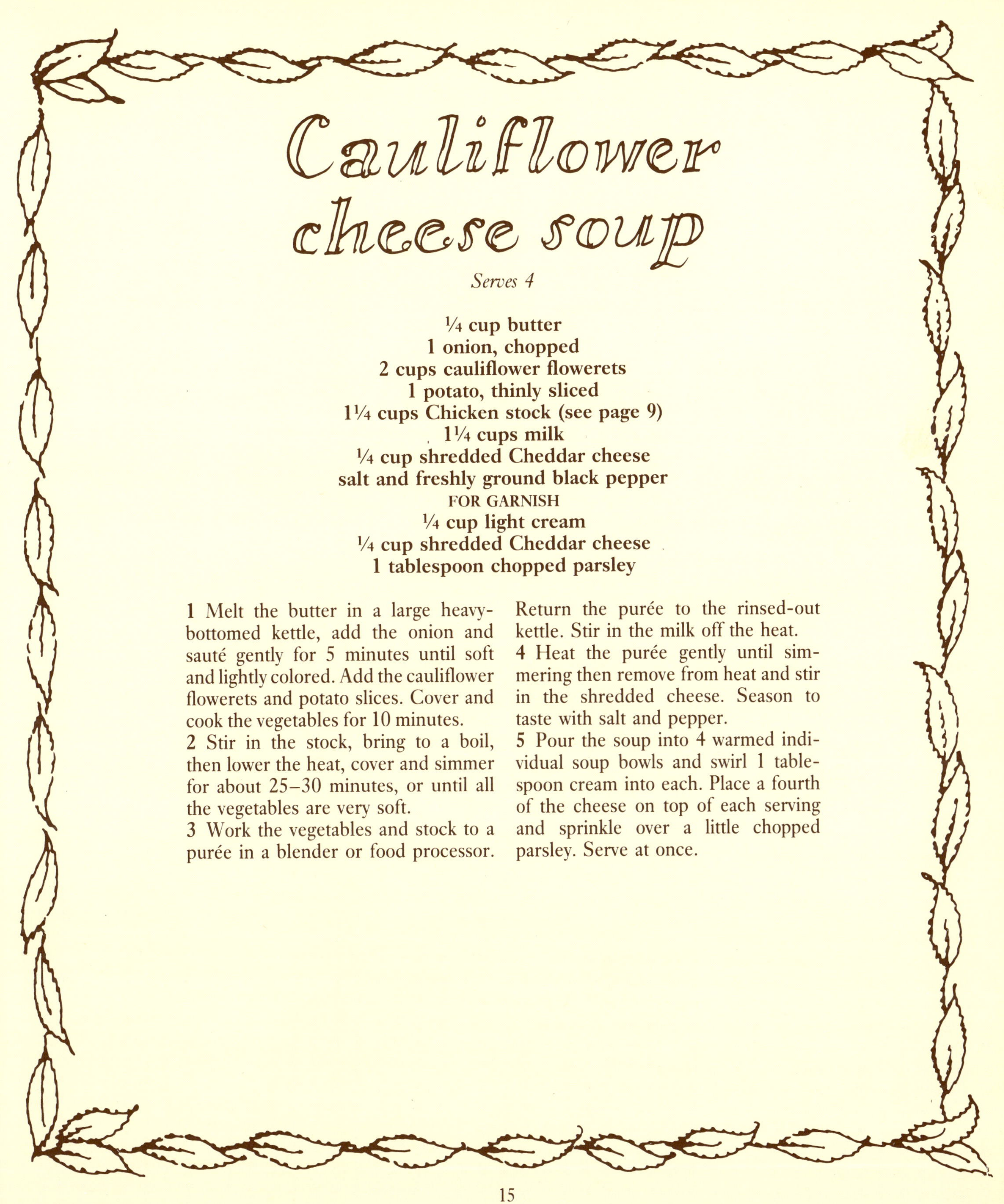

Cauliflower cheese soup

Serves 4

¼ cup butter
1 onion, chopped
2 cups cauliflower flowerets
1 potato, thinly sliced
1¼ cups Chicken stock (see page 9)
1¼ cups milk
¼ cup shredded Cheddar cheese
salt and freshly ground black pepper
FOR GARNISH
¼ cup light cream
¼ cup shredded Cheddar cheese
1 tablespoon chopped parsley

1 Melt the butter in a large heavy-bottomed kettle, add the onion and sauté gently for 5 minutes until soft and lightly colored. Add the cauliflower flowerets and potato slices. Cover and cook the vegetables for 10 minutes.
2 Stir in the stock, bring to a boil, then lower the heat, cover and simmer for about 25–30 minutes, or until all the vegetables are very soft.
3 Work the vegetables and stock to a purée in a blender or food processor. Return the purée to the rinsed-out kettle. Stir in the milk off the heat.
4 Heat the purée gently until simmering then remove from heat and stir in the shredded cheese. Season to taste with salt and pepper.
5 Pour the soup into 4 warmed individual soup bowls and swirl 1 tablespoon cream into each. Place a fourth of the cheese on top of each serving and sprinkle over a little chopped parsley. Serve at once.

Cheese & tomato soup

Serves 4

¼ cup vegetable oil
1 onion, thinly sliced
6 tomatoes, thinly sliced
1 bay leaf, crumbled
½ teaspoon mild paprika
4 cups Chicken stock (see page 9)
salt and freshly ground black pepper
¼ cup cooked rice
2 tablespoons softened butter or margarine
1 cup finely shredded Dutch cheese or Monterey Jack
2 eggs
1 tablespoon lemon juice
1 tablespoon finely chopped chives

1 Heat the oil in a large heavy-bottomed saucepan, add the onion and sauté gently for about 10 minutes until it is soft and lightly colored. Add tomatoes, bay leaf and paprika and sauté for 2 minutes more.
2 Add stock and season with salt and pepper. Bring to a boil, lower the heat, cover the pan and simmer for 1 hour.
3 Strain into a clean saucepan. Stir in the cooked rice and return to the simmering point.
4 In a small bowl, beat soft butter, cheese and eggs until well combined. Stir about 1 cup hot soup into the mixture, then return to the pan. Add lemon juice and adjust seasoning.
5 Divide the soup among 4 warmed individual soup bowls, sprinkle with chives and serve at once.

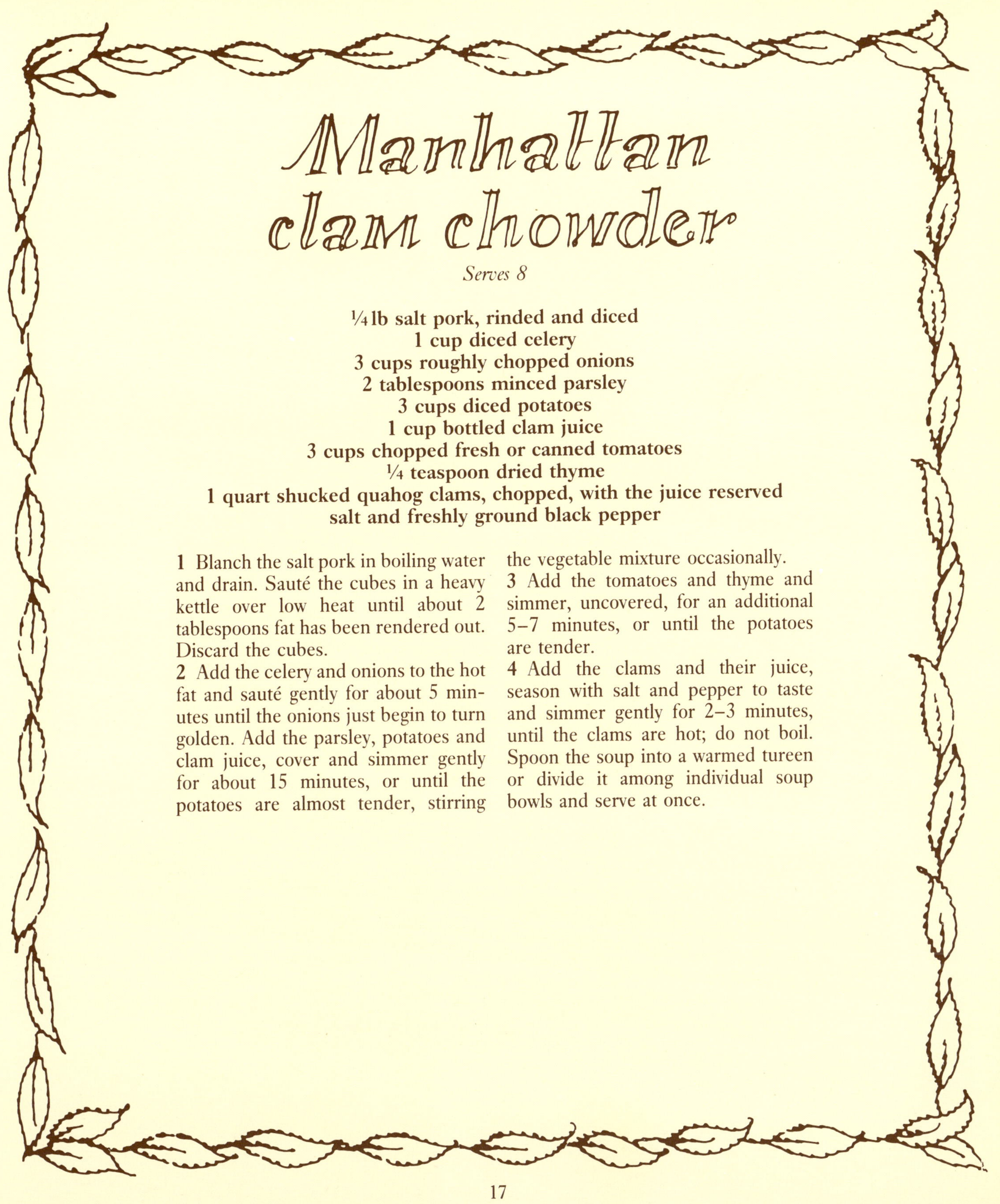

Manhattan clam chowder

Serves 8

¼ lb salt pork, rinded and diced
1 cup diced celery
3 cups roughly chopped onions
2 tablespoons minced parsley
3 cups diced potatoes
1 cup bottled clam juice
3 cups chopped fresh or canned tomatoes
¼ teaspoon dried thyme
1 quart shucked quahog clams, chopped, with the juice reserved
salt and freshly ground black pepper

1 Blanch the salt pork in boiling water and drain. Sauté the cubes in a heavy kettle over low heat until about 2 tablespoons fat has been rendered out. Discard the cubes.

2 Add the celery and onions to the hot fat and sauté gently for about 5 minutes until the onions just begin to turn golden. Add the parsley, potatoes and clam juice, cover and simmer gently for about 15 minutes, or until the potatoes are almost tender, stirring the vegetable mixture occasionally.

3 Add the tomatoes and thyme and simmer, uncovered, for an additional 5–7 minutes, or until the potatoes are tender.

4 Add the clams and their juice, season with salt and pepper to taste and simmer gently for 2–3 minutes, until the clams are hot; do not boil. Spoon the soup into a warmed tureen or divide it among individual soup bowls and serve at once.

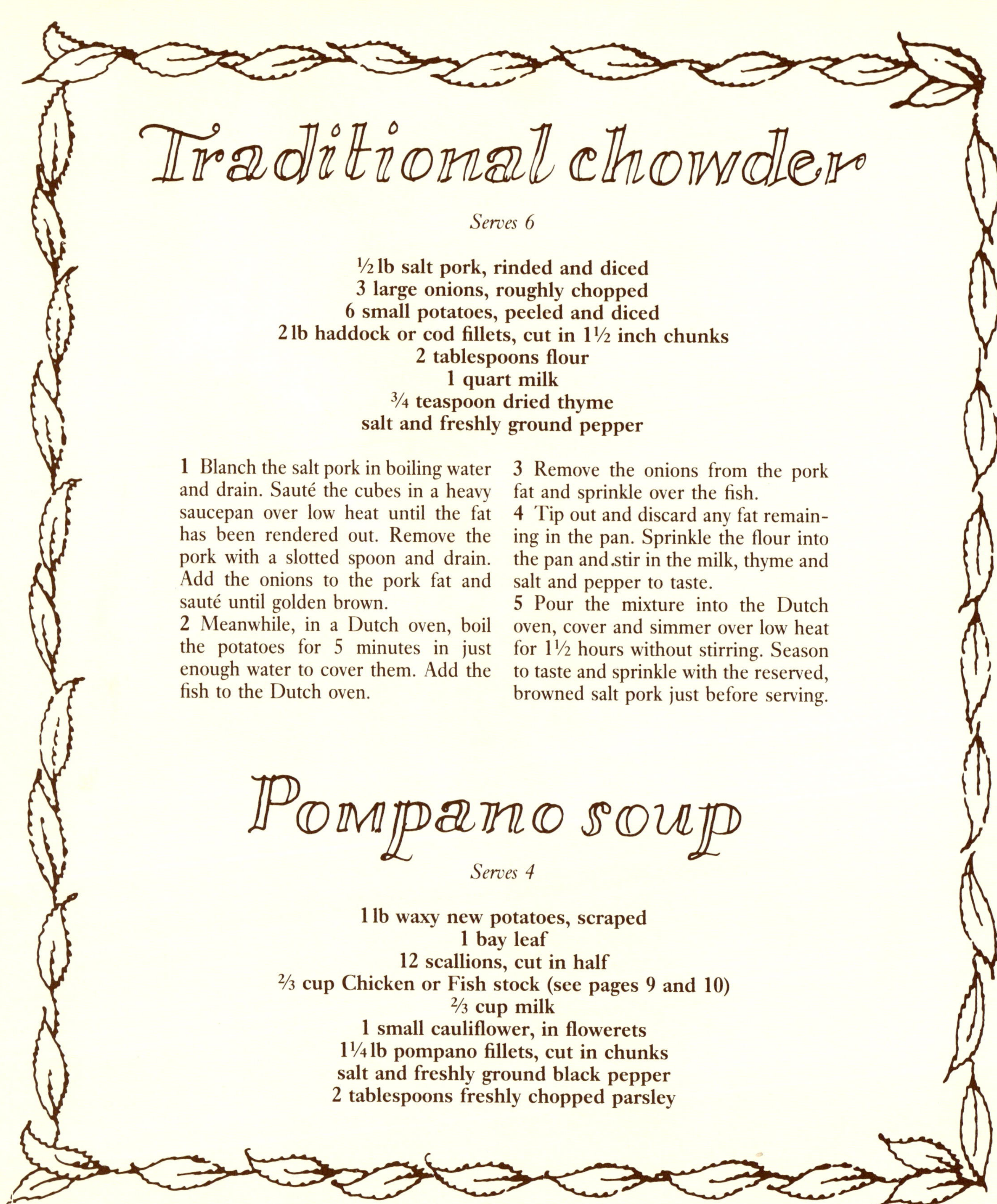

Traditional chowder

Serves 6

½ lb salt pork, rinded and diced
3 large onions, roughly chopped
6 small potatoes, peeled and diced
2 lb haddock or cod fillets, cut in 1½ inch chunks
2 tablespoons flour
1 quart milk
¾ teaspoon dried thyme
salt and freshly ground pepper

1 Blanch the salt pork in boiling water and drain. Sauté the cubes in a heavy saucepan over low heat until the fat has been rendered out. Remove the pork with a slotted spoon and drain. Add the onions to the pork fat and sauté until golden brown.
2 Meanwhile, in a Dutch oven, boil the potatoes for 5 minutes in just enough water to cover them. Add the fish to the Dutch oven.
3 Remove the onions from the pork fat and sprinkle over the fish.
4 Tip out and discard any fat remaining in the pan. Sprinkle the flour into the pan and stir in the milk, thyme and salt and pepper to taste.
5 Pour the mixture into the Dutch oven, cover and simmer over low heat for 1½ hours without stirring. Season to taste and sprinkle with the reserved, browned salt pork just before serving.

Pompano soup

Serves 4

1 lb waxy new potatoes, scraped
1 bay leaf
12 scallions, cut in half
⅔ cup Chicken or Fish stock (see pages 9 and 10)
⅔ cup milk
1 small cauliflower, in flowerets
1¼ lb pompano fillets, cut in chunks
salt and freshly ground black pepper
2 tablespoons freshly chopped parsley

1 Put the potatoes, bay leaf and scallions in a large kettle with the stock. Bring to a boil, lower the heat, cover and simmer for 5 minutes.
2 Add the milk and return to a boil. Add the cauliflower; lower the heat and simmer for 5 minutes more.
3 Add the pompano chunks and salt and pepper to taste, then simmer for 10–15 minutes, until the fish and vegetables are tender.
4 Spoon the soup into a warmed tureen, sprinkle with the chopped parsley and serve at once.

Corn & tuna chowder

Serves 4–6

1 can (11 oz) whole kernel corn
1 can (6½ oz) chunk-light tuna
2 tablespoons butter
1 large onion, minced
2 tablespoons all-purpose flour
2 teaspoons mild paprika
pinch of cayenne
1 quart milk
pinch of salt
grated rind of ½ lemon
TO FINISH
½ cup shredded Cheddar cheese
4 tablespoons chopped parsley

1 Drain the corn, reserving the juice. Drain off the oil from the tuna and discard. Place the fish on kitchen paper towels to remove excess oil. Flake the fish into a bowl.
2 Melt the butter in a saucepan, add the onion and sauté gently until soft but not colored.
3 Stir in the flour, paprika and pinch of cayenne. Cook for 1 minute, stirring constantly with a wooden spoon. Gradually stir in 1¼ cups milk and the reserved corn juice. Now bring the mixture to a boil, stirring constantly.
4 Stir in the remaining milk and bring the mixture to the simmering point. Add the pinch of salt and the grated lemon rind.
5 Add the corn and simmer the soup, uncovered, for 5 minutes. Add the tuna and simmer for 5 minutes more until heated through.
6 To finish: Taste and adjust seasoning, then pour into warmed individual soup bowls. Sprinkle with the cheese and parsley and serve at once..

Mussel soup

Serves 4

2 tablespoons vegetable oil
2 tablespoons butter
1 large onion, minced
1 clove garlic, minced
3 tablespoons minced fresh cilantro or parsley
3 cups water
⅔ cup white wine
1 can (8 oz) tomatoes, drained and chopped
salt and freshly ground black pepper
3 quarts scrubbed bearded unshucked mussels

1 Heat the oil and butter in a large heavy-bottomed kettle, add the onion, the garlic, and the cilantro and sauté gently for about 5 minutes until the onion is soft and lightly colored.
2 Pour in the water and wine and add the tomatoes. Season to taste with salt and pepper.
3 Add the mussels and bring to a boil. Cover the pan, lower the heat and simmer gently for about 10 minutes or until the mussel shells have opened. Discard any mussels that do not open during cooking.
4 Snap off empty half-shells and put mussels into a warmed soup tureen or divide among individual soup bowls. Spoon soup over and serve at once.

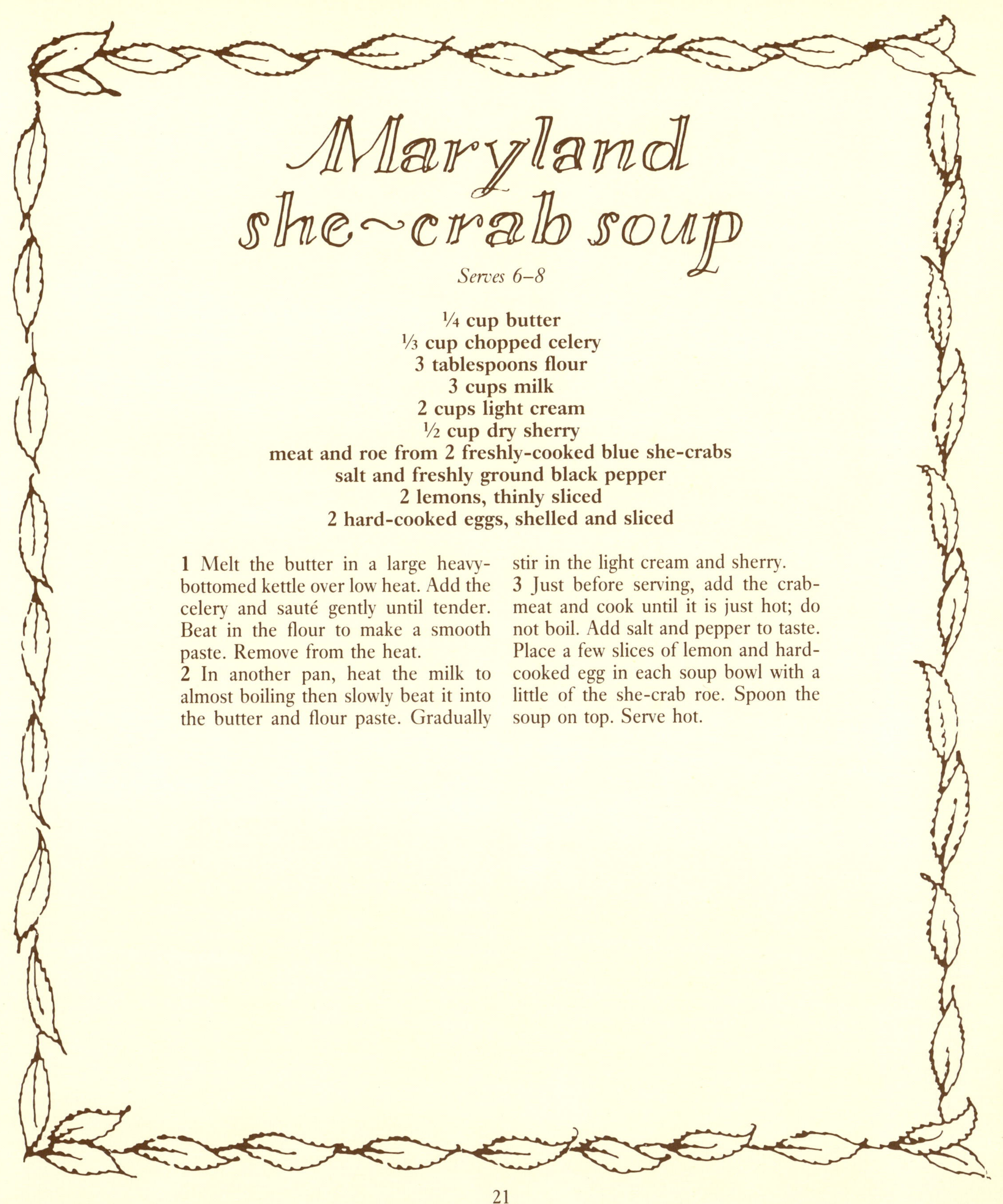

Maryland she-crab soup

Serves 6–8

¼ cup butter
⅓ cup chopped celery
3 tablespoons flour
3 cups milk
2 cups light cream
½ cup dry sherry
meat and roe from 2 freshly-cooked blue she-crabs
salt and freshly ground black pepper
2 lemons, thinly sliced
2 hard-cooked eggs, shelled and sliced

1 Melt the butter in a large heavy-bottomed kettle over low heat. Add the celery and sauté gently until tender. Beat in the flour to make a smooth paste. Remove from the heat.

2 In another pan, heat the milk to almost boiling then slowly beat it into the butter and flour paste. Gradually stir in the light cream and sherry.

3 Just before serving, add the crab-meat and cook until it is just hot; do not boil. Add salt and pepper to taste. Place a few slices of lemon and hard-cooked egg in each soup bowl with a little of the she-crab roe. Spoon the soup on top. Serve hot.

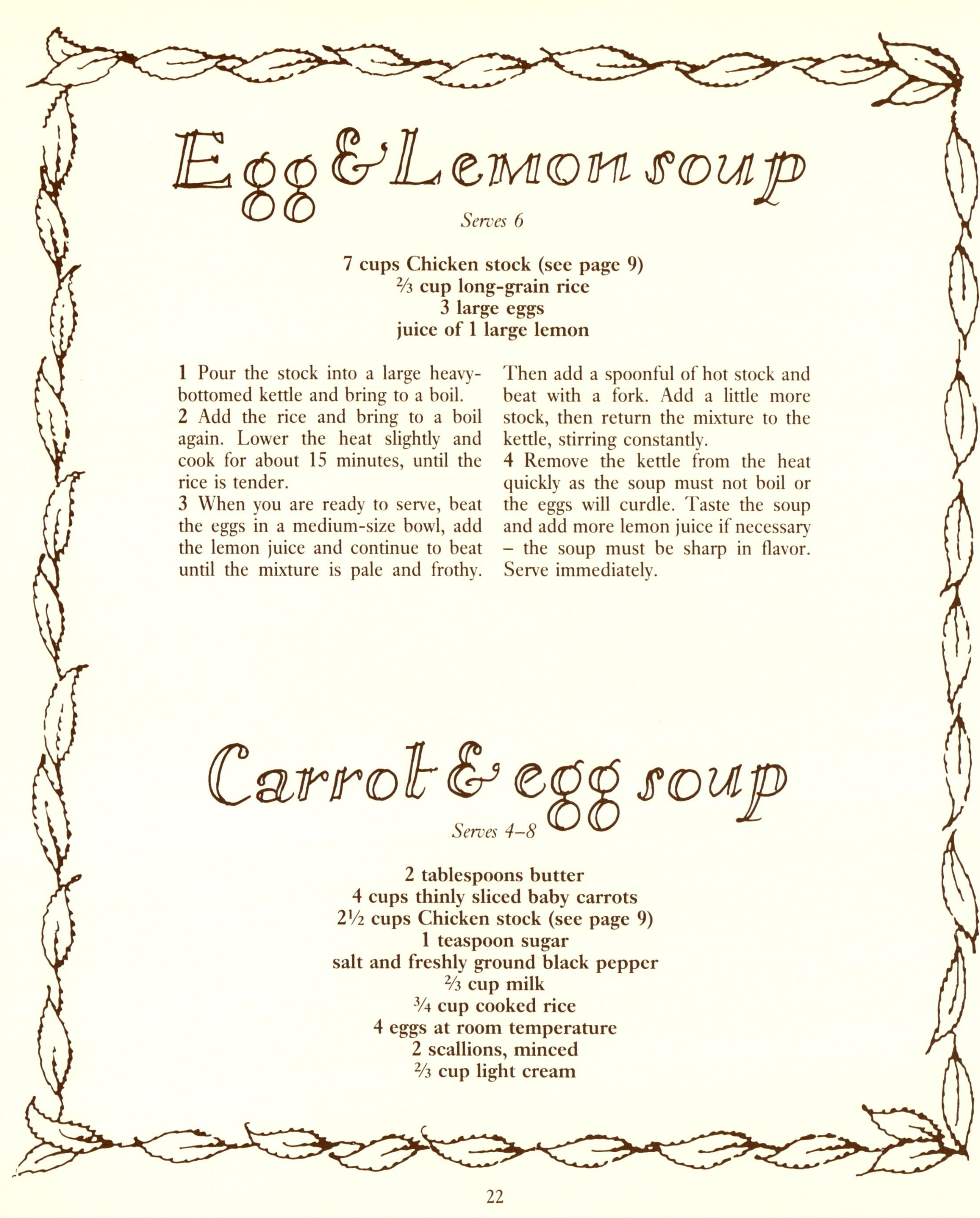

Egg & Lemon soup

Serves 6

7 cups Chicken stock (see page 9)
⅔ cup long-grain rice
3 large eggs
juice of 1 large lemon

1 Pour the stock into a large heavy-bottomed kettle and bring to a boil.

2 Add the rice and bring to a boil again. Lower the heat slightly and cook for about 15 minutes, until the rice is tender.

3 When you are ready to serve, beat the eggs in a medium-size bowl, add the lemon juice and continue to beat until the mixture is pale and frothy. Then add a spoonful of hot stock and beat with a fork. Add a little more stock, then return the mixture to the kettle, stirring constantly.

4 Remove the kettle from the heat quickly as the soup must not boil or the eggs will curdle. Taste the soup and add more lemon juice if necessary – the soup must be sharp in flavor. Serve immediately.

Carrot & egg soup

Serves 4–8

2 tablespoons butter
4 cups thinly sliced baby carrots
2½ cups Chicken stock (see page 9)
1 teaspoon sugar
salt and freshly ground black pepper
⅔ cup milk
¾ cup cooked rice
4 eggs at room temperature
2 scallions, minced
⅔ cup light cream

1 Melt the butter in a saucepan, add the carrots and sauté gently for 2–3 minutes to soften slightly.
2 Add the chicken stock and sugar and season to taste with salt and pepper. Bring to a boil, then lower the heat and simmer, uncovered, for 30 minutes or until the carrots are very tender.
3 Off heat, let mixture cool slightly, then work to a purée in a blender or food processor. Return the purée to the rinsed-out pan and stir in the milk and the cooked rice. Taste and adjust the seasoning, if necessary.
4 Heat the soup gently until hot but not boiling, then break in the eggs and poach them for about 8 minutes or until they are firm enough to be lifted out with a slotted spoon.
5 Spoon an egg into each of 4 warmed soup bowls and carefully pour over the soup. Sprinkle over the scallions, swirl in the cream and serve at once.

Caraway soup with egg dumplings

Serves 8

2 tablespoons flour
8 cups Beef or Chicken stock (see pages 9 and 10)
2 tablespoons caraway seeds
2 tablespoons vegetable oil
½ cup cold water
DUMPLINGS
1 egg
3–4 tablespoons flour
¼ teaspoon salt

1 In a small saucepan, lightly brown the flour, stirring constantly. Set aside.
2 Pour the stock and caraway seeds into a large kettle and bring to a boil. Lower the heat and simmer seeds for 30 minutes, then strain, discarding seeds.
3 In a small bowl, mix the browned flour with the oil. When smooth, stir in the water. Add this mixture to the caraway broth, stirring rapidly and bring to a boil.
4 Make the dumplings: In a large bowl, beat the egg with a fork. Add the flour and salt, beating the flour mixture constantly.
5 Drop the dumpling batter by teaspoonfuls into the boiling soup. Lower the heat and simmer for 5 minutes, or until the dumplings are cooked through. Divide the soup and dumplings among 8 warmed individual soup bowls and serve at once.

Meat & Poultry Soups

Beef, pork, lamb and bacon – even the humble sausage – make filling, nourishing and warming soups. The specially selected recipes in this chapter produce wonderful contrasts of texture and flavor, enhanced with blends of herbs and spices; many of these soups make perfect one-pot meals. Nourishing oxtail, with its array of vegetables, is sure to be a favorite while the spicy lamb soup, stewed slowly with beans, peas and lentils is wonderfully appetizing. These substantial soups are filling enough to simply be accompanied with hunks of crusty wholewheat or garlic bread, followed by fresh fruit.

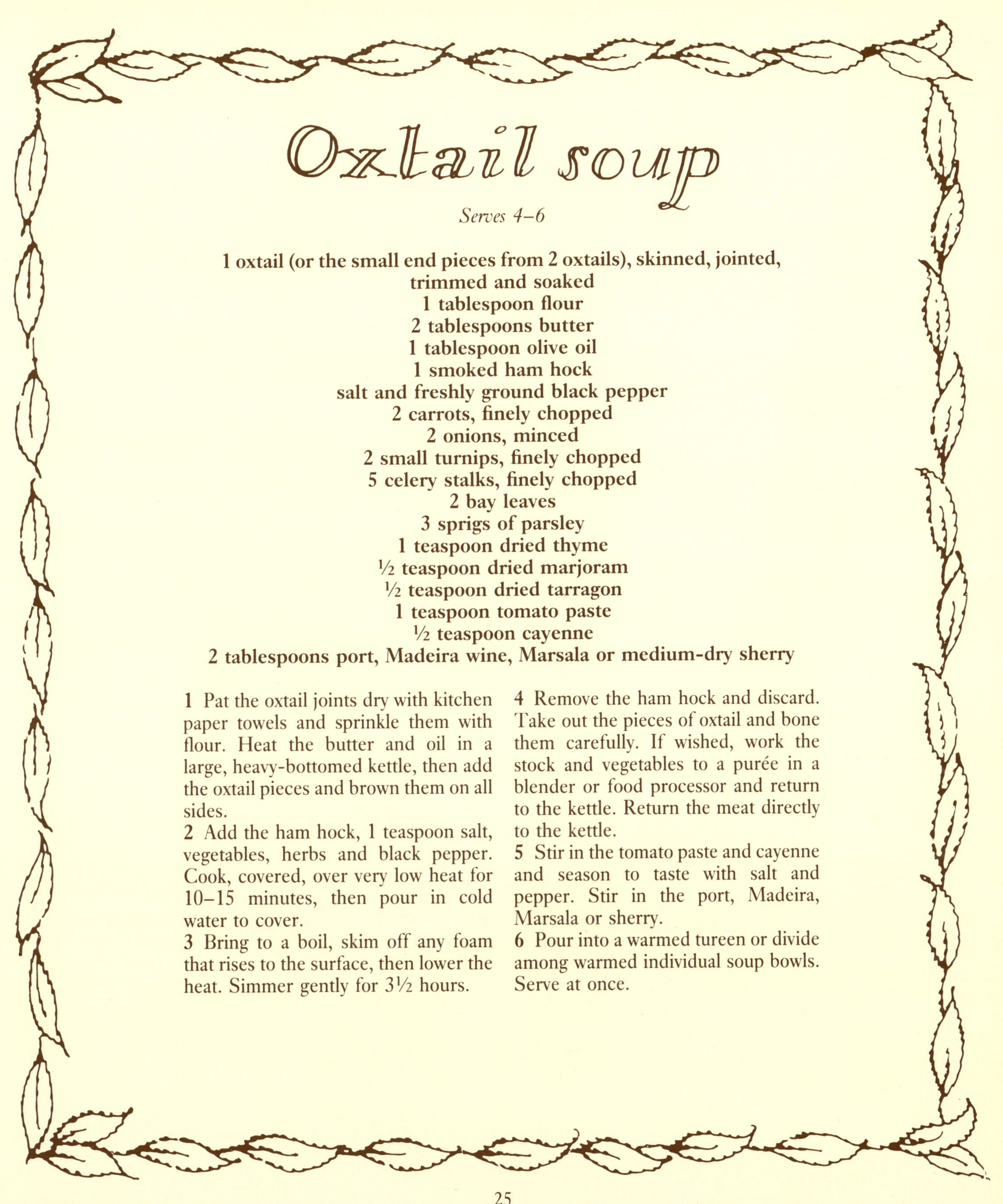

Oxtail soup

Serves 4–6

1 oxtail (or the small end pieces from 2 oxtails), skinned, jointed, trimmed and soaked
1 tablespoon flour
2 tablespoons butter
1 tablespoon olive oil
1 smoked ham hock
salt and freshly ground black pepper
2 carrots, finely chopped
2 onions, minced
2 small turnips, finely chopped
5 celery stalks, finely chopped
2 bay leaves
3 sprigs of parsley
1 teaspoon dried thyme
½ teaspoon dried marjoram
½ teaspoon dried tarragon
1 teaspoon tomato paste
½ teaspoon cayenne
2 tablespoons port, Madeira wine, Marsala or medium-dry sherry

1 Pat the oxtail joints dry with kitchen paper towels and sprinkle them with flour. Heat the butter and oil in a large, heavy-bottomed kettle, then add the oxtail pieces and brown them on all sides.

2 Add the ham hock, 1 teaspoon salt, vegetables, herbs and black pepper. Cook, covered, over very low heat for 10–15 minutes, then pour in cold water to cover.

3 Bring to a boil, skim off any foam that rises to the surface, then lower the heat. Simmer gently for 3½ hours.

4 Remove the ham hock and discard. Take out the pieces of oxtail and bone them carefully. If wished, work the stock and vegetables to a purée in a blender or food processor and return to the kettle. Return the meat directly to the kettle.

5 Stir in the tomato paste and cayenne and season to taste with salt and pepper. Stir in the port, Madeira, Marsala or sherry.

6 Pour into a warmed tureen or divide among warmed individual soup bowls. Serve at once.

Chili soup

Serves 4

1 tablespoon corn oil
1 large onion, chopped
¾ cup lean ground beef
½ teaspoon ground cumin
1 tablespoon all-purpose flour
1 can (8 oz) tomatoes
½ teaspoon hot pepper sauce or chili powder
1 quart Beef stock (see page 10)
salt and freshly ground black pepper
1 can (16 oz) red kidney beans, drained
fresh cilantro or flat-leaved parsley, for garnish (optional)

1 Heat the oil in a saucepan and add the onion, ground beef and cumin. Cook over a high heat until the meat is evenly browned, stirring with a wooden spoon and mix thoroughly.

2 Sprinkle in the flour and stir well, then add the tomatoes with their juice, the hot pepper sauce or chili powder and the stock.

3 Bring to a boil, stirring. Season to taste with salt and freshly ground black pepper. Lower the heat and simmer, uncovered, for 25 minutes.

4 Stir in the drained beans and cook for 5 minutes more or until heated through. Transfer to a warmed tureen or divide among warmed individual soup bowls and serve at once.

Oriental beef & spinach

Serves 6–8

½ lb chuck or blade beef, thinly sliced and cut in 1 inch cubes
2 scallions, chopped
1 garlic clove, chopped
5 tablespoons soy sauce
1 teaspoon salt and freshly ground black pepper
9 cups water
1 tablespoon sesame seeds
4 cups shredded spinach

1 Put the beef in a large heavy-bottomed kettle with the scallions, garlic, soy sauce, salt and pepper and mix well. Cook over medium high-heat for a few minutes until the meat is browned on all sides.
2 Add the water and simmer gently for a few minutes, remove any foam, add the sesame seeds and continue cooking for 35 minutes or until the meat is tender.
3 Just before serving, add the shredded spinach. Simmer for 2–5 minutes or until tender.
4 Pour the soup into a warmed tureen or individual soup bowls. Serve at once.

Tomato, beef & tea broth

Serves 6

4 bacon slices, diced
1 large onion, finely chopped
1 cup lean ground beef
4 cups strong tea
4 beef bouillon cubes, crumbled
½ teaspoon dried marjoram
½ teaspoon dried mixed herbs
1 can (16 oz) tomatoes
salt and freshly ground black pepper
croutons, to serve

1 Cook the bacon in a large heavy-bottomed kettle until the fat runs. Add the onion and ground beef and cook gently for 5 minutes, stirring.
2 Add the tea, bouillon cubes, herbs, tomatoes with their juice and salt and pepper to taste. Bring to a boil, lower the heat and simmer for 15 minutes, stirring occasionally.
3 Pour into a warmed tureen or divide among warmed individual soup bowls. Serve with croutons.

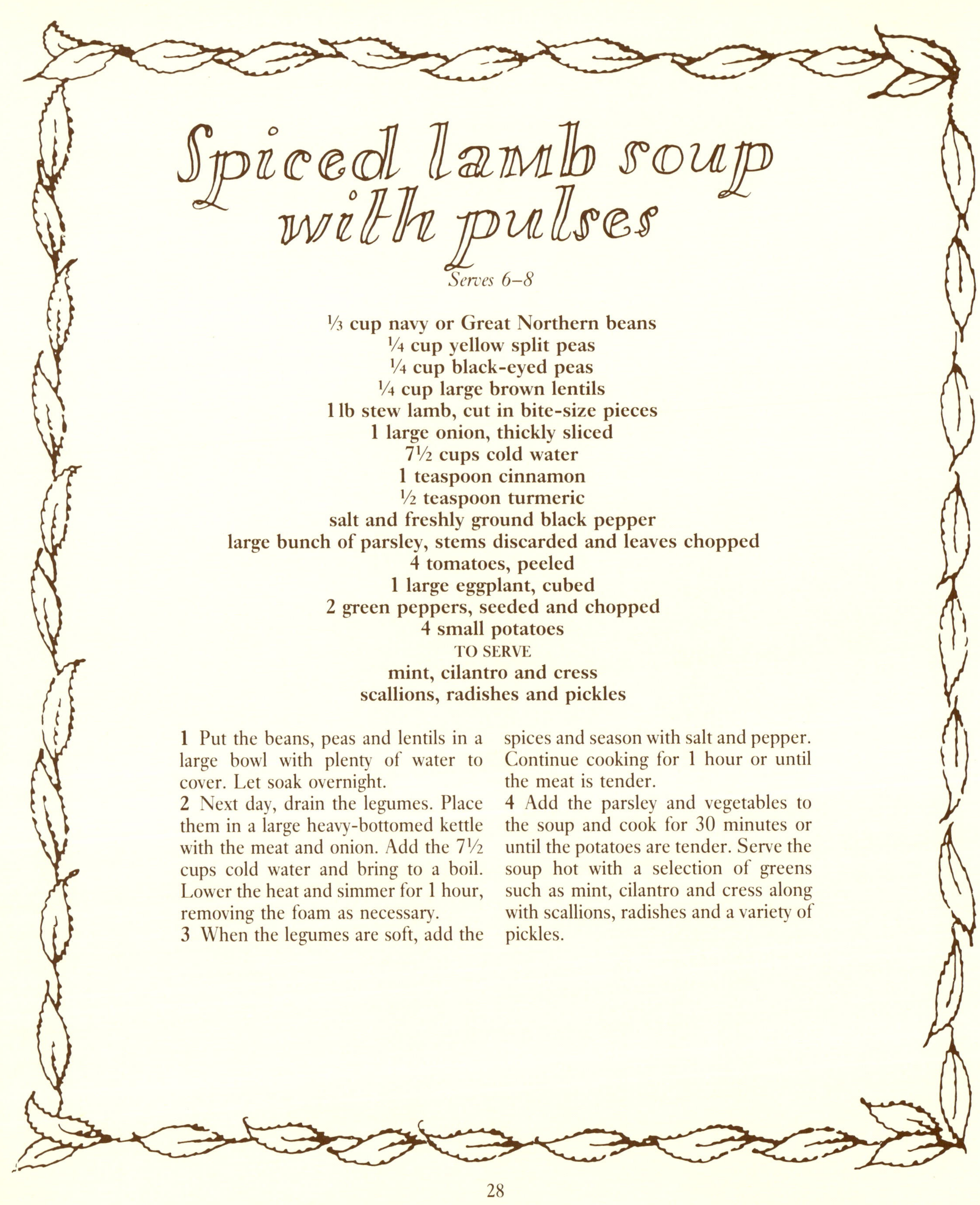

Spiced lamb soup with pulses

Serves 6–8

⅓ cup navy or Great Northern beans
¼ cup yellow split peas
¼ cup black-eyed peas
¼ cup large brown lentils
1 lb stew lamb, cut in bite-size pieces
1 large onion, thickly sliced
7½ cups cold water
1 teaspoon cinnamon
½ teaspoon turmeric
salt and freshly ground black pepper
large bunch of parsley, stems discarded and leaves chopped
4 tomatoes, peeled
1 large eggplant, cubed
2 green peppers, seeded and chopped
4 small potatoes
TO SERVE
mint, cilantro and cress
scallions, radishes and pickles

1 Put the beans, peas and lentils in a large bowl with plenty of water to cover. Let soak overnight.

2 Next day, drain the legumes. Place them in a large heavy-bottomed kettle with the meat and onion. Add the 7½ cups cold water and bring to a boil. Lower the heat and simmer for 1 hour, removing the foam as necessary.

3 When the legumes are soft, add the spices and season with salt and pepper. Continue cooking for 1 hour or until the meat is tender.

4 Add the parsley and vegetables to the soup and cook for 30 minutes or until the potatoes are tender. Serve the soup hot with a selection of greens such as mint, cilantro and cress along with scallions, radishes and a variety of pickles.

Bean & ham soup

Serves 4–6

2¼ cups dried navy or Great Northern beans
1 onion, quartered
1 carrot, roughly chopped
1 garlic clove, minced
1 bouquet garni
9 cups cold water
½ lb smoked shoulder butt or cottage ham, in one piece
⅔ cup heavy cream
¼ cup chilled butter, in small pieces
salt (optional)
1 tablespoon chopped fresh chervil or 1 teaspoon dried chervil, for garnish

1 Put the beans in a large bowl with plenty of cold water. Let soak overnight.

2 Next day, drain the beans and place them in a large heavy-bottomed kettle with the onion, carrot, garlic and bouquet garni. Pour in the 9 cups cold water and bring to a boil. Add the smoked ham, lower the heat and simmer for 1¼–1½ hours until the beans are cooked.

3 Remove the bouquet garni and smoked ham. Chop the ham in small cubes and reserve them.

4 Work the vegetables and liquid to a purée in a blender or food processor and return to the rinsed-out kettle. Reheat the mixture gently. Add the cream and pieces of butter, stirring until thoroughly blended.

5 Add the cubed ham and reheat gently. Taste and add salt if required – the smoked ham may make this unnecessary. Pour the soup into a warmed tureen or divide among individual soup bowls and serve at once, sprinkled with the chervil.

Ham & pasta soup

Serves 4

1 tablespoon olive oil
1 onion, chopped
4 small carrots, sliced
3 stalks celery, sliced
2 large tomatoes, blanched, peeled, seeded and chopped
½ cup chopped mushrooms
6 cups Ham stock (see Variation, page 9)
1 cup chopped cooked country ham
¾ cup small pasta shells
½ teaspoon oregano
salt and freshly ground black pepper

1 Heat the oil in a large heavy-bottomed saucepan and add the onion, carrots and celery. Sauté over low heat for about 5 minutes until the onion is soft and lightly colored.

2 Add the tomatoes, mushrooms and stock, bring to a boil, lower the heat and simmer mixture for 20 minutes.

3 Stir in the cooked ham, pasta shells, oregano, salt and freshly ground black pepper, and simmer 15 minutes more.

4 Pour into a warmed tureen or divide among warmed individual soup bowls. Serve at once.

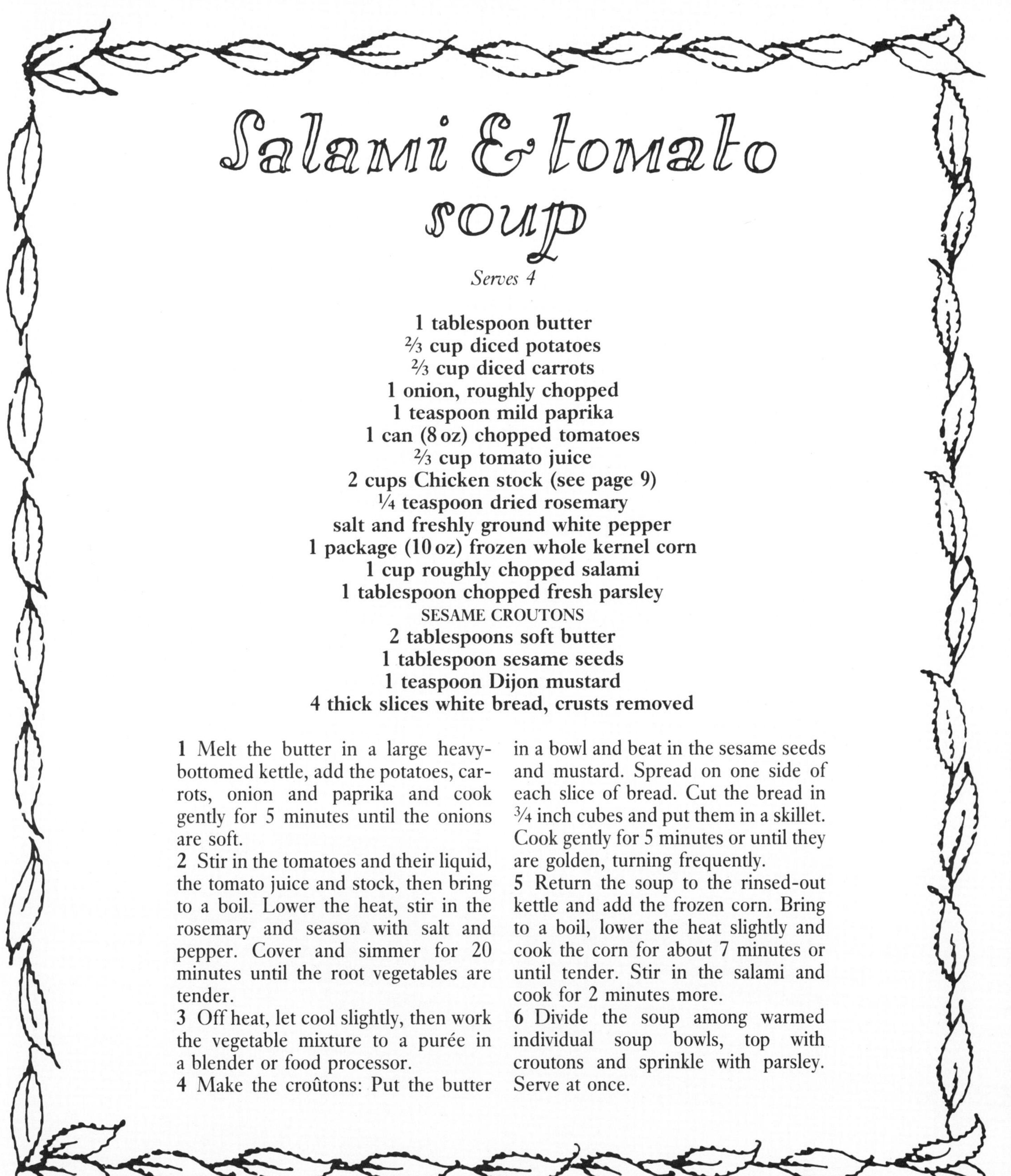

Salami & tomato soup

Serves 4

1 tablespoon butter
⅔ cup diced potatoes
⅔ cup diced carrots
1 onion, roughly chopped
1 teaspoon mild paprika
1 can (8 oz) chopped tomatoes
⅔ cup tomato juice
2 cups Chicken stock (see page 9)
¼ teaspoon dried rosemary
salt and freshly ground white pepper
1 package (10 oz) frozen whole kernel corn
1 cup roughly chopped salami
1 tablespoon chopped fresh parsley
SESAME CROUTONS
2 tablespoons soft butter
1 tablespoon sesame seeds
1 teaspoon Dijon mustard
4 thick slices white bread, crusts removed

1 Melt the butter in a large heavy-bottomed kettle, add the potatoes, carrots, onion and paprika and cook gently for 5 minutes until the onions are soft.

2 Stir in the tomatoes and their liquid, the tomato juice and stock, then bring to a boil. Lower the heat, stir in the rosemary and season with salt and pepper. Cover and simmer for 20 minutes until the root vegetables are tender.

3 Off heat, let cool slightly, then work the vegetable mixture to a purée in a blender or food processor.

4 Make the croûtons: Put the butter in a bowl and beat in the sesame seeds and mustard. Spread on one side of each slice of bread. Cut the bread in ¾ inch cubes and put them in a skillet. Cook gently for 5 minutes or until they are golden, turning frequently.

5 Return the soup to the rinsed-out kettle and add the frozen corn. Bring to a boil, lower the heat slightly and cook the corn for about 7 minutes or until tender. Stir in the salami and cook for 2 minutes more.

6 Divide the soup among warmed individual soup bowls, top with croutons and sprinkle with parsley. Serve at once.

Country soup

Serves 4

1 potato, diced
1 large onion, sliced
1 small head celery, sliced
¼ head firm cabbage, shredded
1 can (8 oz) tomatoes
1 quart Beef stock (see page 10)
1 package (10 oz) frozen peas
1 large or 2 medium frankfurters
⅓ cup diced garlic sausage or salami
⅓ cup diced smoked sausage
salt and freshly ground black pepper
1 tablespoon minced fresh parsley

1 Put the potato, onion, celery and cabbage in a large heavy-bottomed kettle. Add the tomatoes with their juice, breaking them up against the side of the kettle with a wooden spoon.

2 Add the stock to the pan and bring quickly to a boil. Lower the heat, cover and simmer for 40 minutes.

3 Add the peas, cover and cook for 5 minutes more.

4 Meanwhile, bring a pan of water to a boil. Add the frankfurters and heat them through for 2 minutes. Remove with a slotted spoon and slice.

5 Add the garlic sausage and smoked sausage and the frankfurters to the soup. Simmer over a low heat for 15 minutes. Taste and adjust seasoning, if necessary, then pour into a warmed tureen or divide among warmed individual soup bowls and sprinkle with chopped parsley. Serve at once.

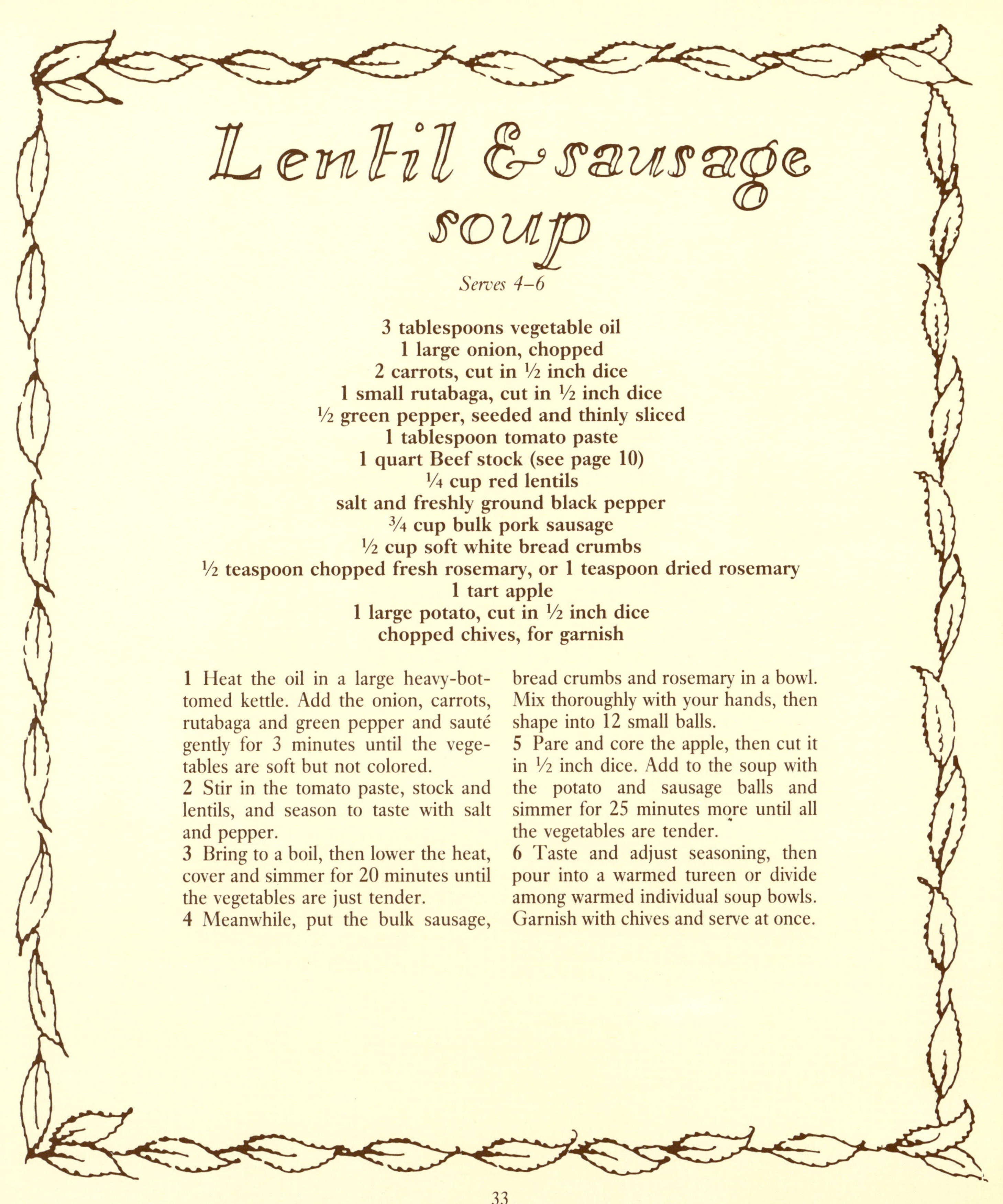

Lentil & sausage soup

Serves 4–6

3 tablespoons vegetable oil
1 large onion, chopped
2 carrots, cut in ½ inch dice
1 small rutabaga, cut in ½ inch dice
½ green pepper, seeded and thinly sliced
1 tablespoon tomato paste
1 quart Beef stock (see page 10)
¼ cup red lentils
salt and freshly ground black pepper
¾ cup bulk pork sausage
½ cup soft white bread crumbs
½ teaspoon chopped fresh rosemary, or 1 teaspoon dried rosemary
1 tart apple
1 large potato, cut in ½ inch dice
chopped chives, for garnish

1 Heat the oil in a large heavy-bottomed kettle. Add the onion, carrots, rutabaga and green pepper and sauté gently for 3 minutes until the vegetables are soft but not colored.

2 Stir in the tomato paste, stock and lentils, and season to taste with salt and pepper.

3 Bring to a boil, then lower the heat, cover and simmer for 20 minutes until the vegetables are just tender.

4 Meanwhile, put the bulk sausage, bread crumbs and rosemary in a bowl. Mix thoroughly with your hands, then shape into 12 small balls.

5 Pare and core the apple, then cut it in ½ inch dice. Add to the soup with the potato and sausage balls and simmer for 25 minutes more until all the vegetables are tender.

6 Taste and adjust seasoning, then pour into a warmed tureen or divide among warmed individual soup bowls. Garnish with chives and serve at once.

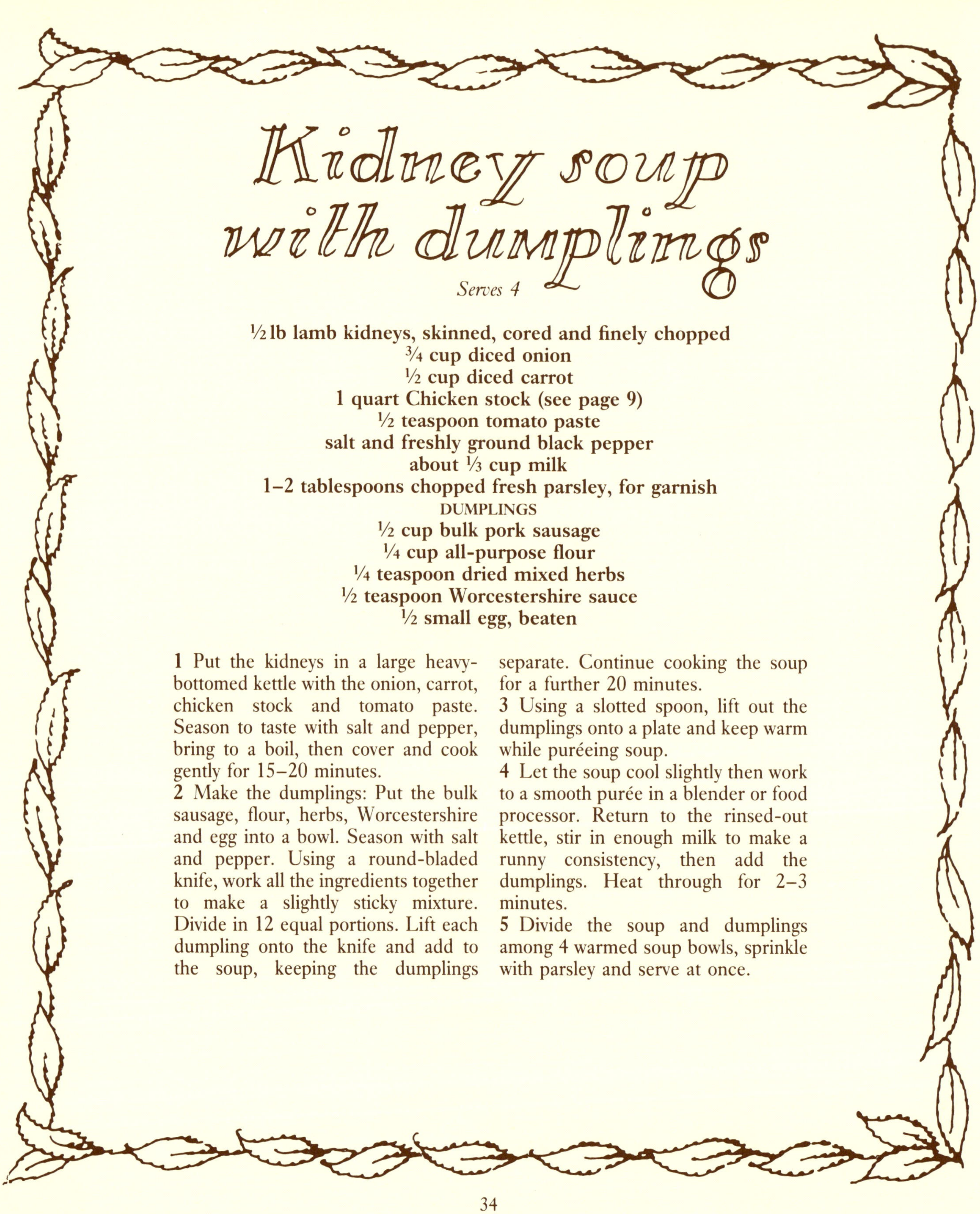

Kidney soup with dumplings

Serves 4

½ lb lamb kidneys, skinned, cored and finely chopped
¾ cup diced onion
½ cup diced carrot
1 quart Chicken stock (see page 9)
½ teaspoon tomato paste
salt and freshly ground black pepper
about ⅓ cup milk
1–2 tablespoons chopped fresh parsley, for garnish

DUMPLINGS

½ cup bulk pork sausage
¼ cup all-purpose flour
¼ teaspoon dried mixed herbs
½ teaspoon Worcestershire sauce
½ small egg, beaten

1 Put the kidneys in a large heavy-bottomed kettle with the onion, carrot, chicken stock and tomato paste. Season to taste with salt and pepper, bring to a boil, then cover and cook gently for 15–20 minutes.

2 Make the dumplings: Put the bulk sausage, flour, herbs, Worcestershire and egg into a bowl. Season with salt and pepper. Using a round-bladed knife, work all the ingredients together to make a slightly sticky mixture. Divide in 12 equal portions. Lift each dumpling onto the knife and add to the soup, keeping the dumplings separate. Continue cooking the soup for a further 20 minutes.

3 Using a slotted spoon, lift out the dumplings onto a plate and keep warm while puréeing soup.

4 Let the soup cool slightly then work to a smooth purée in a blender or food processor. Return to the rinsed-out kettle, stir in enough milk to make a runny consistency, then add the dumplings. Heat through for 2–3 minutes.

5 Divide the soup and dumplings among 4 warmed soup bowls, sprinkle with parsley and serve at once.

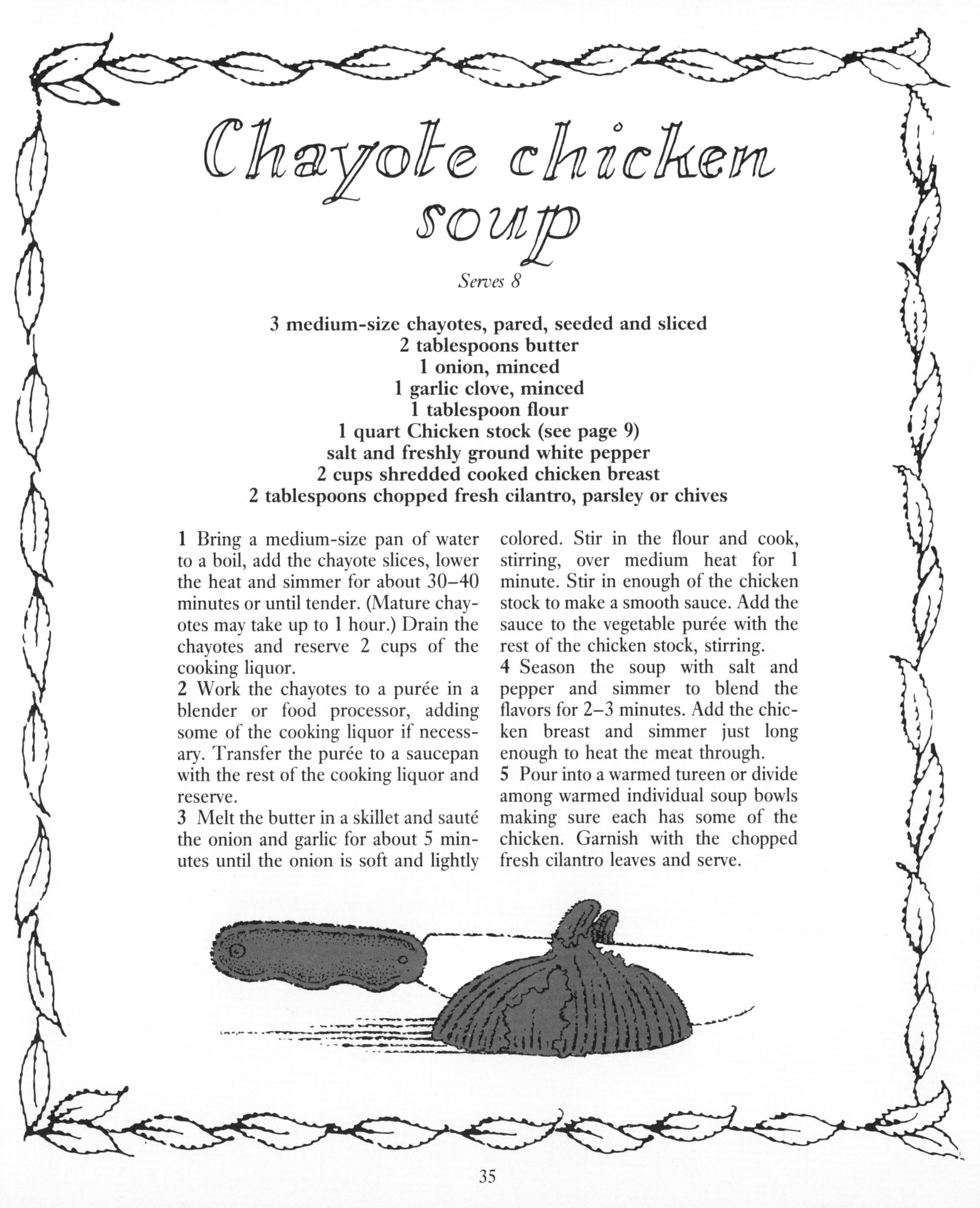

Chayote chicken soup

Serves 8

3 medium-size chayotes, pared, seeded and sliced
2 tablespoons butter
1 onion, minced
1 garlic clove, minced
1 tablespoon flour
1 quart Chicken stock (see page 9)
salt and freshly ground white pepper
2 cups shredded cooked chicken breast
2 tablespoons chopped fresh cilantro, parsley or chives

1 Bring a medium-size pan of water to a boil, add the chayote slices, lower the heat and simmer for about 30–40 minutes or until tender. (Mature chayotes may take up to 1 hour.) Drain the chayotes and reserve 2 cups of the cooking liquor.

2 Work the chayotes to a purée in a blender or food processor, adding some of the cooking liquor if necessary. Transfer the purée to a saucepan with the rest of the cooking liquor and reserve.

3 Melt the butter in a skillet and sauté the onion and garlic for about 5 minutes until the onion is soft and lightly colored. Stir in the flour and cook, stirring, over medium heat for 1 minute. Stir in enough of the chicken stock to make a smooth sauce. Add the sauce to the vegetable purée with the rest of the chicken stock, stirring.

4 Season the soup with salt and pepper and simmer to blend the flavors for 2–3 minutes. Add the chicken breast and simmer just long enough to heat the meat through.

5 Pour into a warmed tureen or divide among warmed individual soup bowls making sure each has some of the chicken. Garnish with the chopped fresh cilantro leaves and serve.

Chicken & vegetable soup

Serves 4

4 cups Chicken stock (see page 9)
1 large carrot, shredded
1 turnip or rutabaga, shredded
2 leeks, trimmed and shredded
1½ cups shredded cabbage
½ cup shredded cooked chicken
2 tablespoons minced fresh parsley
salt and finely ground black pepper
shredded Cheddar cheese, to serve

1 Pour the stock into a large heavy-bottomed saucepan, and bring to a boil. Add the carrot, turnip or rutabaga, leeks and cabbage. Lower the heat and simmer for 15 minutes.

2 Add the chicken and parsley and simmer for 5 minutes more or until the vegetables are cooked.

3 Season to taste and serve in a warmed tureen or warmed individual soup bowls. When serving, pass the shredded cheese separately.

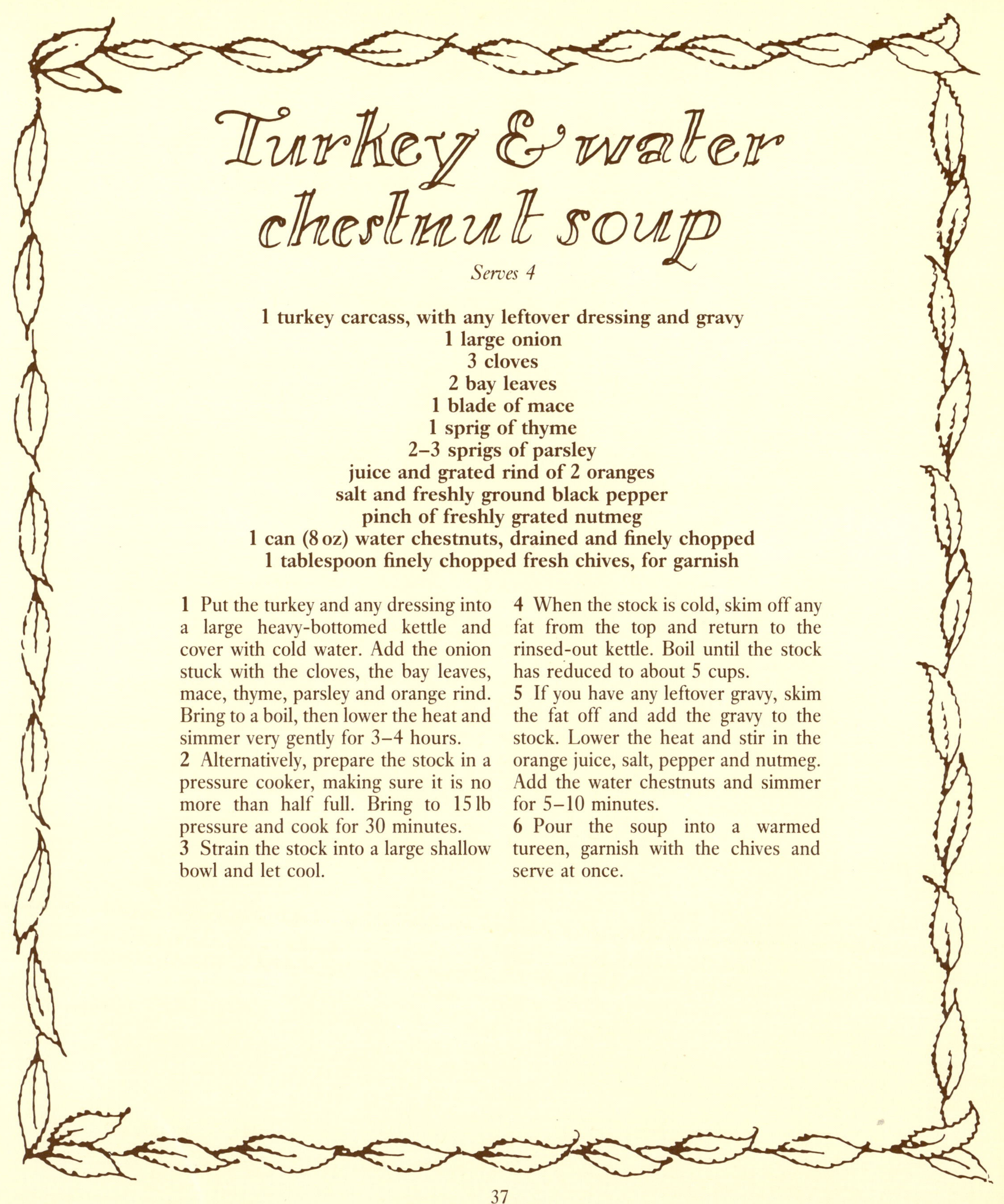

Turkey & water chestnut soup

Serves 4

1 turkey carcass, with any leftover dressing and gravy
1 large onion
3 cloves
2 bay leaves
1 blade of mace
1 sprig of thyme
2–3 sprigs of parsley
juice and grated rind of 2 oranges
salt and freshly ground black pepper
pinch of freshly grated nutmeg
1 can (8 oz) water chestnuts, drained and finely chopped
1 tablespoon finely chopped fresh chives, for garnish

1 Put the turkey and any dressing into a large heavy-bottomed kettle and cover with cold water. Add the onion stuck with the cloves, the bay leaves, mace, thyme, parsley and orange rind. Bring to a boil, then lower the heat and simmer very gently for 3–4 hours.

2 Alternatively, prepare the stock in a pressure cooker, making sure it is no more than half full. Bring to 15 lb pressure and cook for 30 minutes.

3 Strain the stock into a large shallow bowl and let cool.

4 When the stock is cold, skim off any fat from the top and return to the rinsed-out kettle. Boil until the stock has reduced to about 5 cups.

5 If you have any leftover gravy, skim the fat off and add the gravy to the stock. Lower the heat and stir in the orange juice, salt, pepper and nutmeg. Add the water chestnuts and simmer for 5–10 minutes.

6 Pour the soup into a warmed tureen, garnish with the chives and serve at once.

Vegetable Soups

Colorful, cheering, chunky or smooth, vegetable soups are an excellent way to make the most of seasonal crops. In this section delicious soups are conjured up from the humblest of ingredients which, when gently simmered with stock and seasoning, come to the table full of goodness and with mouth-watering aromas. Some of the vegetable soups are topped off with crusty croutons or pastry coverings for extra 'bite'; others are light and clear, ideal as a warming snack or opener. These vegetable soups are full of wholesome, country ingredients and, because you eat the cooking liquor along with the vegetables, none of the precious nutrients are lost.

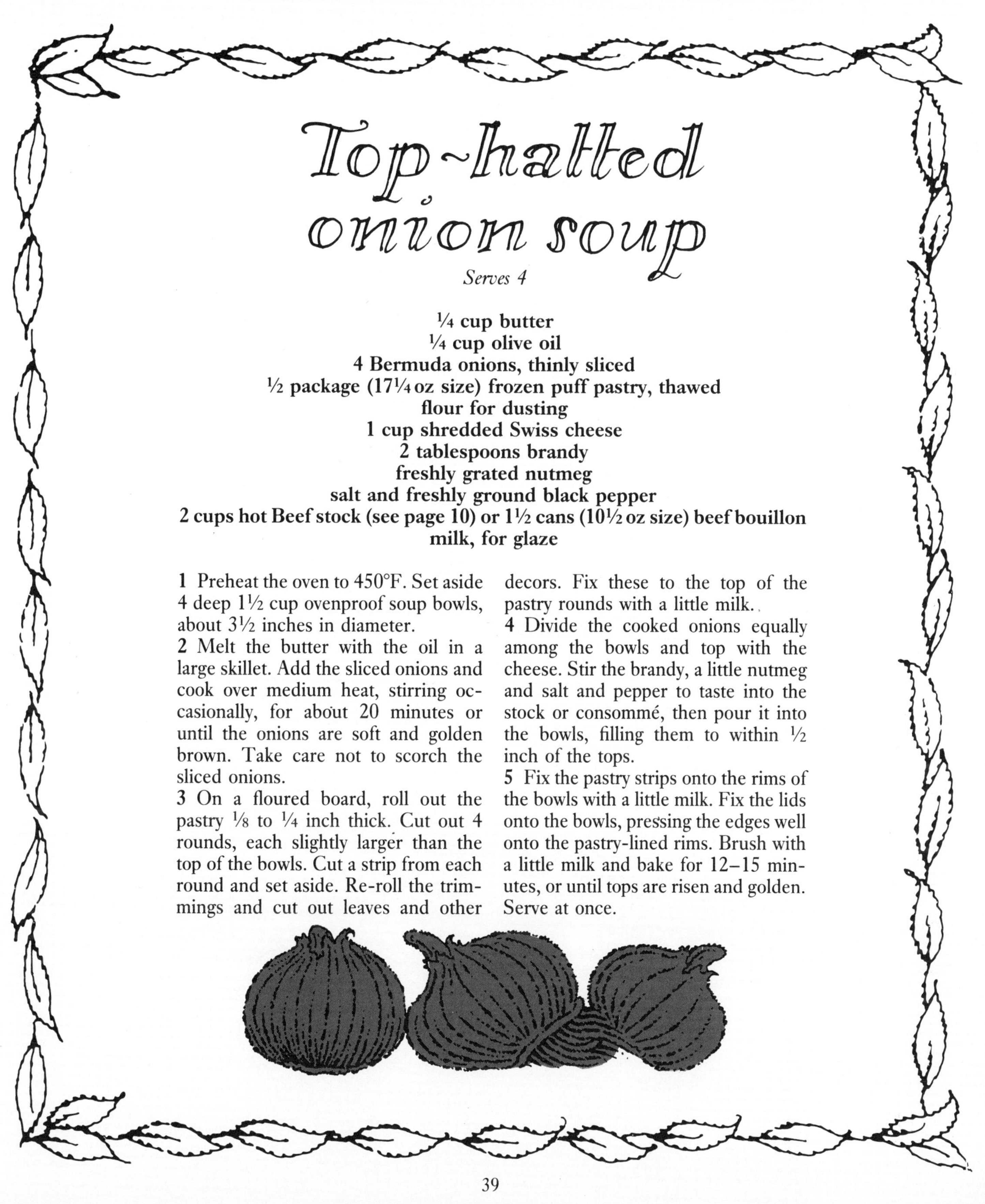

Top-hatted onion soup

Serves 4

¼ cup butter
¼ cup olive oil
4 Bermuda onions, thinly sliced
½ package (17¼ oz size) frozen puff pastry, thawed
flour for dusting
1 cup shredded Swiss cheese
2 tablespoons brandy
freshly grated nutmeg
salt and freshly ground black pepper
2 cups hot Beef stock (see page 10) or 1½ cans (10½ oz size) beef bouillon
milk, for glaze

1 Preheat the oven to 450°F. Set aside 4 deep 1½ cup ovenproof soup bowls, about 3½ inches in diameter.

2 Melt the butter with the oil in a large skillet. Add the sliced onions and cook over medium heat, stirring occasionally, for about 20 minutes or until the onions are soft and golden brown. Take care not to scorch the sliced onions.

3 On a floured board, roll out the pastry ⅛ to ¼ inch thick. Cut out 4 rounds, each slightly larger than the top of the bowls. Cut a strip from each round and set aside. Re-roll the trimmings and cut out leaves and other decors. Fix these to the top of the pastry rounds with a little milk.

4 Divide the cooked onions equally among the bowls and top with the cheese. Stir the brandy, a little nutmeg and salt and pepper to taste into the stock or consommé, then pour it into the bowls, filling them to within ½ inch of the tops.

5 Fix the pastry strips onto the rims of the bowls with a little milk. Fix the lids onto the bowls, pressing the edges well onto the pastry-lined rims. Brush with a little milk and bake for 12–15 minutes, or until tops are risen and golden. Serve at once.

Clear turnip soup

Serves 4

1 quart Chicken stock (see page 9)
1 lb baby turnips, cut in batons
¼ cup butter
2 cloves garlic, minced
salt and freshly ground black pepper
1 cup fried croutons
1 cup shredded Swiss cheese

1 Pour the stock into a large saucepan and bring to a boil. Add turnip batons and blanch for 2 minutes. Drain well, reserving blanching liquor.
2 Melt the butter in a heavy-bottomed saucepan over low heat until it foams. Add garlic and sauté over low heat for 1 minute. Add the turnip batons and cook for about 4 minutes, turning occasionally until golden and tender.
3 Heat the reserved blanching liquid and season. Divide the croutons between 4 warmed soup plates. Pour the liquid into soup plates, spoon in the turnip batons and sprinkle with the cheese. Serve hot.

Sweet potato soup

Serves 6

1 lb white sweet potatoes, pared and sliced
salt
¼ cup butter
1 onion, minced
1 lb tomatoes, peeled and chopped
2 small fresh red or green hot chilies, seeded and chopped, or red pepper sauce to taste
1 quart Chicken stock (see page 9)
2 tablespoons chopped fresh parsley, or cilantro

1 Put the sweet potato slices into a saucepan with salted water to cover. Bring to a boil, lower the heat and cook, covered, for about 20 minutes or until tender. Drain and roughly chop.
2 Melt the butter in a skillet over low

heat and sauté the onion until it is soft. Add the tomatoes and chilies and cook for 5 minutes more. Work the onion and tomato mixture with the sweet potatoes and 1 cup of the chicken stock to a purée using a blender or food processor.

3 Transfer the purée to a kettle. Stir in the rest of the stock. Taste for seasoning and add salt if necessary. Simmer over low heat for 2 minutes to blend the flavors.

4 Pour the soup into a warmed tureen or divide among 6 warmed individual soup bowls and sprinkle with parsley or cilantro. Serve at once.

Eggplant soup

Serves 4–6

1 tablespoon oil
1 large onion, chopped
1 tablespoon dry sherry
1 eggplant (about 1 lb), chopped
2 cups diced potatoes
2 beef bouillon cubes
1 tablespoon tomato paste
1 bay leaf
½ teaspoon oregano
salt and freshly ground black pepper
1 quart water
2–3 tablespoons milk
croutons to serve

1 Heat the oil in a heavy-bottomed kettle. Add the chopped onion and sauté for 2–3 minutes, then add the sherry and bring to a boil.

2 Add the eggplant, potatoes, bouillon cubes, tomato paste, bay leaf, oregano, salt and pepper and the water. Bring to a boil, then lower the heat, cover and simmer for 45 minutes.

3 Work the soup to a purée in a blender or food processor, return it to the rinsed-out pan and reheat gradually. Stir the milk into the soup and heat through until warmed thoroughly.

4 Pour the soup into a warmed tureen or divide among warmed individual soup bowls. Serve at once, garnished with the croutons.

Creamed chestnut soup

Serves 4

2 tablespoons butter
1 large onion, minced
4 large celery stalks, finely chopped
½ lb sweet chestnuts, boiled, peeled and minced
1 quart Chicken stock (see page 9)
½ teaspoon ground mace
1 bouquet garni
salt and freshly ground black pepper
¼ cup heavy cream
2 tablespoons chopped parsley

1 Melt the butter in a large heavy-bottomed kettle over low heat. Add the onion and celery, cover and cook gently for 10 minutes.
2 Stir the chestnuts into the kettle. Pour in the stock and bring to the boil. Add the mace and bouquet garni and season. Lower the heat and simmer, uncovered, for 15 minutes.
3 Let the soup cool slightly, then work it to a purée in a blender or food processor and then return it to the rinsed-out kettle.
4 Reheat the soup gently. Serve in warmed individual soup bowls with a swirl of heavy cream and a sprinkling of chopped parsley on top of each bowl of soup.

Fennel soup

Serves 4–6

2 medium-size fennel bulbs
¼ cup walnut oil
7½ cups Chicken stock (see page 9)
salt and freshly ground black pepper
⅔ cup heavy cream
1 teaspoon Pernod

1 Trim any feathery fronds from the top of the fennel bulbs, chop finely and reserve, for garnish. Wash and finely chop the bulbs, discarding any bruised or discolored layers.
2 Heat the oil in a heavy-bottomed kettle, add the chopped fennel and sauté for 2 minutes over medium heat. Lower the heat and cook gently for 10 minutes.
3 Stir in the chicken stock, bring to a boil, lower heat and simmer for 15–20 minutes or until the fennel is tender. Remove from heat and let cool.
4 When cool work the fennel and stock to a purée in a blender or food processor. Return to the rinsed-out kettle and reheat gently.
5 Add salt and pepper to taste, and just before serving stir in the cream and the Pernod. Pour into a warmed tureen or warmed individual soup bowls, garnish with the reserved feathery fronds and serve immediately.

Creamy mushroom soup

Serves 4

½ lb button mushrooms, wiped clean
¼ cup butter
2 tablespoons all-purpose flour
2½ cups milk
1 package (3 oz) cream cheese
2 tablespoons chopped chives
2 teaspoons lemon juice
salt and freshly ground black pepper

1 Finely chop the mushrooms, reserving 2–3 whole ones for the garnish. Melt half the butter in a skillet. Add the chopped mushrooms and sauté for about 5 minutes. Set aside.
2 Melt the remaining butter in a large saucepan, sprinkle in flour and stir over low heat for 1–2 minutes until it is straw-colored. Off heat, gradually stir in milk. Return to the heat and simmer, stirring, until the mixture is thick and smooth.
3 Remove from the heat again and add the cheese, a little at a time, stirring until melted. Stir in half the chives, all the mushrooms, their juices and the lemon juice. Season to taste. Return to heat and simmer for 2–3 minutes. Do not allow to boil.
4 Pour into 4 warmed soup bowls. Float a few slices of mushrooms on top of each serving. Sprinkle lightly with the remaining chives and serve the soup at once.

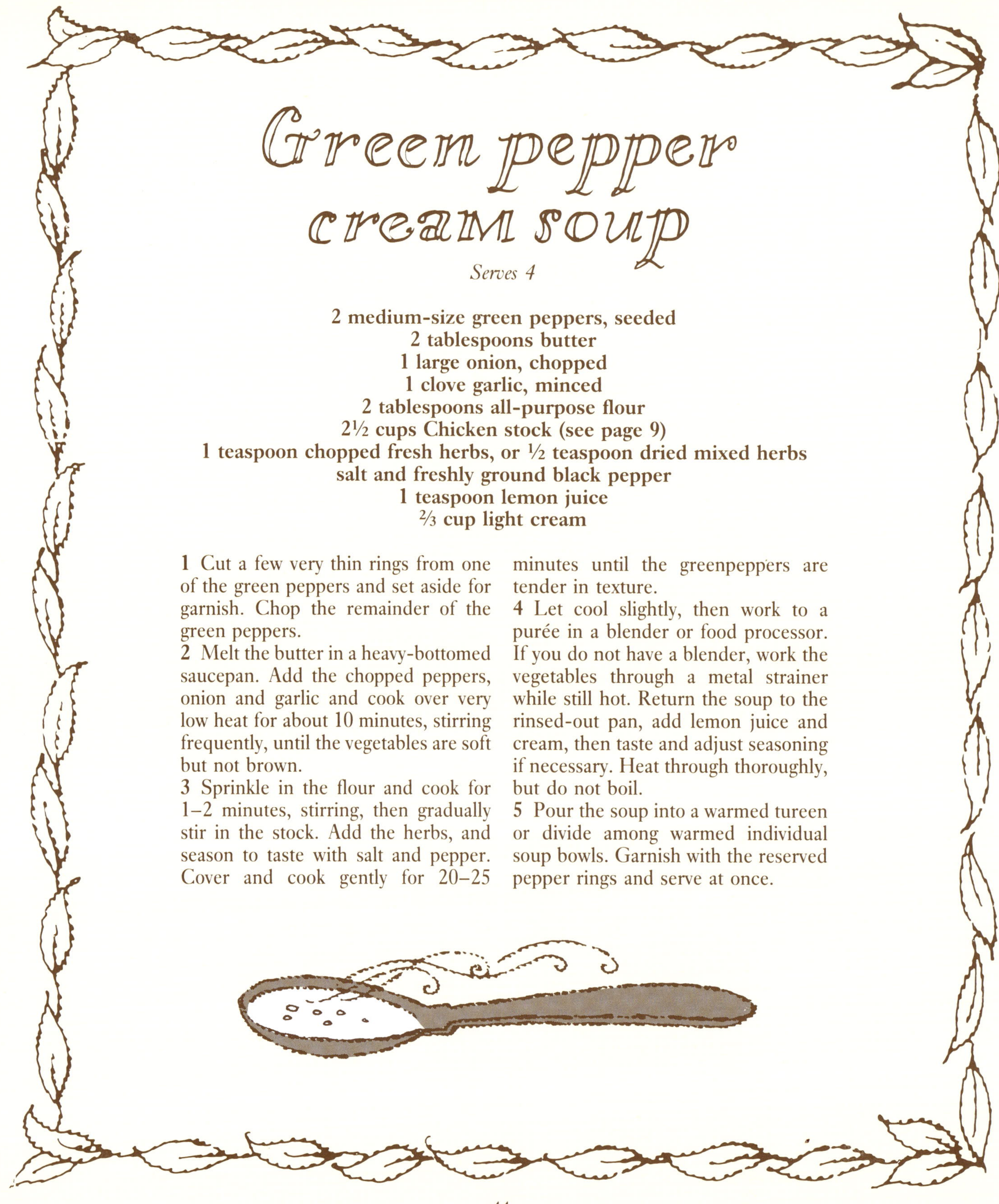

Green pepper cream soup

Serves 4

2 medium-size green peppers, seeded
2 tablespoons butter
1 large onion, chopped
1 clove garlic, minced
2 tablespoons all-purpose flour
2½ cups Chicken stock (see page 9)
1 teaspoon chopped fresh herbs, or ½ teaspoon dried mixed herbs
salt and freshly ground black pepper
1 teaspoon lemon juice
⅔ cup light cream

1 Cut a few very thin rings from one of the green peppers and set aside for garnish. Chop the remainder of the green peppers.

2 Melt the butter in a heavy-bottomed saucepan. Add the chopped peppers, onion and garlic and cook over very low heat for about 10 minutes, stirring frequently, until the vegetables are soft but not brown.

3 Sprinkle in the flour and cook for 1–2 minutes, stirring, then gradually stir in the stock. Add the herbs, and season to taste with salt and pepper. Cover and cook gently for 20–25 minutes until the greenpeppers are tender in texture.

4 Let cool slightly, then work to a purée in a blender or food processor. If you do not have a blender, work the vegetables through a metal strainer while still hot. Return the soup to the rinsed-out pan, add lemon juice and cream, then taste and adjust seasoning if necessary. Heat through thoroughly, but do not boil.

5 Pour the soup into a warmed tureen or divide among warmed individual soup bowls. Garnish with the reserved pepper rings and serve at once.

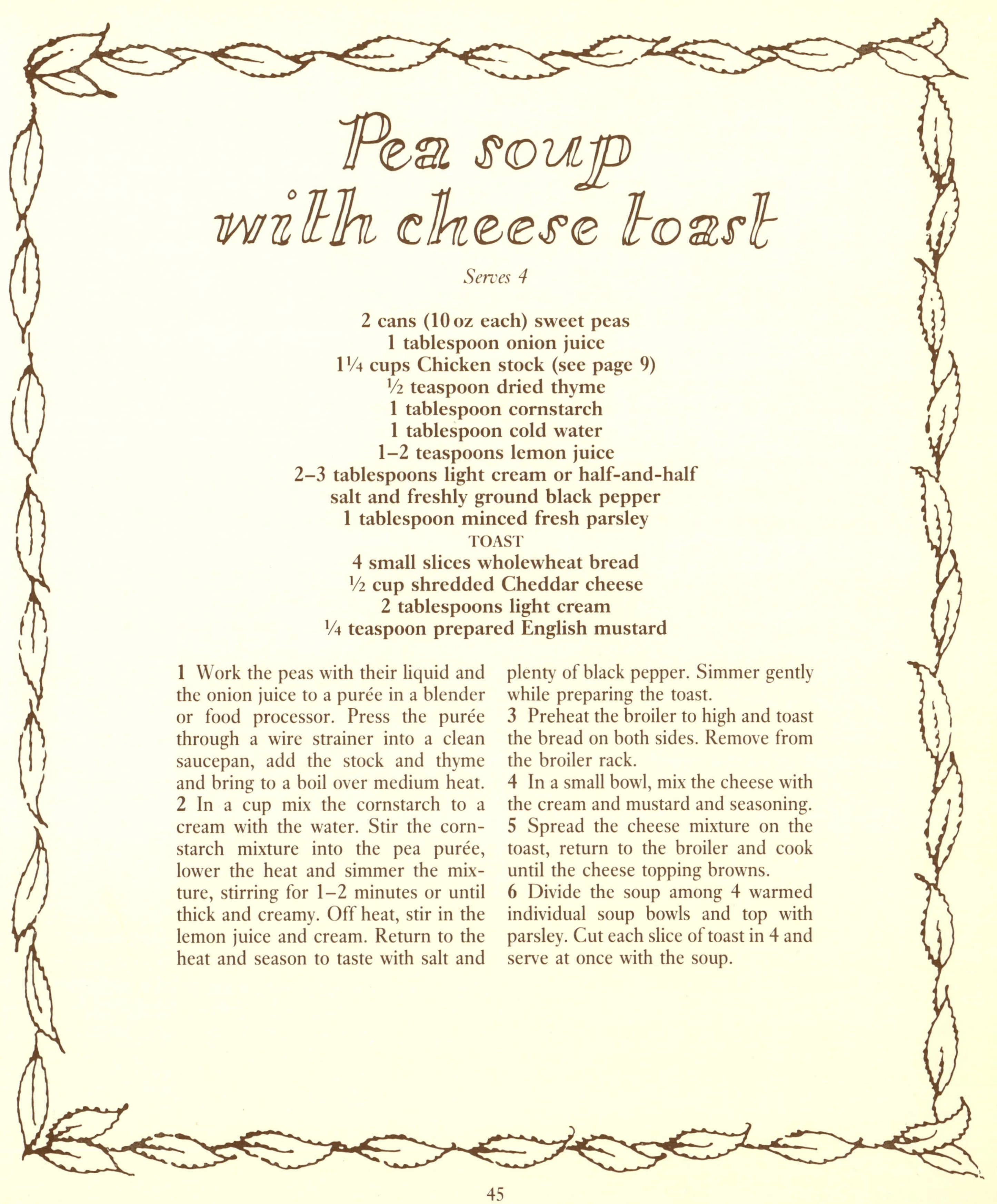

Pea soup with cheese toast

Serves 4

2 cans (10 oz each) sweet peas
1 tablespoon onion juice
1¼ cups Chicken stock (see page 9)
½ teaspoon dried thyme
1 tablespoon cornstarch
1 tablespoon cold water
1–2 teaspoons lemon juice
2–3 tablespoons light cream or half-and-half
salt and freshly ground black pepper
1 tablespoon minced fresh parsley

TOAST

4 small slices wholewheat bread
½ cup shredded Cheddar cheese
2 tablespoons light cream
¼ teaspoon prepared English mustard

1 Work the peas with their liquid and the onion juice to a purée in a blender or food processor. Press the purée through a wire strainer into a clean saucepan, add the stock and thyme and bring to a boil over medium heat.

2 In a cup mix the cornstarch to a cream with the water. Stir the cornstarch mixture into the pea purée, lower the heat and simmer the mixture, stirring for 1–2 minutes or until thick and creamy. Off heat, stir in the lemon juice and cream. Return to the heat and season to taste with salt and plenty of black pepper. Simmer gently while preparing the toast.

3 Preheat the broiler to high and toast the bread on both sides. Remove from the broiler rack.

4 In a small bowl, mix the cheese with the cream and mustard and seasoning.

5 Spread the cheese mixture on the toast, return to the broiler and cook until the cheese topping browns.

6 Divide the soup among 4 warmed individual soup bowls and top with parsley. Cut each slice of toast in 4 and serve at once with the soup.

Celery & peanut soup

Serves 4

1 tablespoon butter
1 tablespoon vegetable oil
4 large celery stalks, chopped
1 onion, chopped
3 cups Chicken stock (see page 9)
6 tablespoons crunchy peanut butter
salt and freshly ground black pepper
¼ cup light cream, to serve
chopped celery leaves, for garnish

1 Melt the butter and oil in a saucepan, add the celery and onion and sauté gently for about 5 minutes.
2 Add the stock and bring to a boil. Lower the heat, cover and simmer gently for about 30 minutes until the celery is tender.
3 Cool the mixture a little, then work to a purée in a blender.
4 Return to the rinsed-out pan, place over low heat, then beat in the peanut butter. Heat through until just boiling. Taste and then season with salt and freshly ground black pepper.
5 Divide the soup among 4 warmed individual bowls. Swirl cream on the surface of each, garnish with chopped celery leaves and serve at once.

Leekie oat broth

Serves 4

2½ cups Chicken stock (see page 9)
1 cup thinly sliced leeks
⅔ cup finely diced carrots
½ teaspoon dried mixed herbs
salt and freshly ground black pepper
2 tablespoons old-fashioned oats
⅔ cup milk
2 tablespoons light cream or evaporated milk
1 cup cubed Dutch cheese, for garnish

1 Pour the stock into a saucepan and bring to a boil. Add the leeks, carrots, herbs and salt and pepper to taste. Lower the heat, cover and simmer for 15 minutes or until the vegetables are just tender.
2 Sprinkle the oats into the soup, stir in the milk and cook gently, uncovered, for 5 minutes, stirring from time to time, until thick. Stir in the cream or evaporated milk and heat through, but without allowing the soup to boil.
3 Pour the soup into a warmed tureen or divide it among individual serving bowls. Mix the cubes of Dutch cheese into the soup. Serve at once, before the cheese has completely melted.

Sunshine soup

Serves 6

5 cups diced pumpkin
salt
3 tablespoons butter
1 large onion, minced
2 tomatoes, peeled and chopped
1 teaspoon chopped chives
¼ teaspoon freshly grated nutmeg
1 tablespoon shredded coconut
2½ cups Chicken stock (see page 9)
freshly ground black pepper
1¼ cups light cream
mild paprika, for garnish

1 Put the pumpkin into a saucepan, add enough water just to cover and a pinch of salt. Bring to a boil, then lower the heat slightly and simmer, covered, for 15 minutes. Drain the pumpkin well.
2 Melt the butter in a saucepan, add the onion and sauté gently for 5 minutes until soft and lightly colored.
3 Add the pumpkin, tomatoes, chives, nutmeg and coconut and sauté gently for 5 minutes more.
4 Pour in the stock, season with salt and pepper to taste and bring to a boil. Lower the heat slightly, cover and simmer for about 30 minutes.
5 Off heat, allow the soup to cool slightly, then work to a purée in a blender or food processor. Stir in half the cream.
6 Divide the soup among 6 warmed soup bowls and swirl in the remaining cream. Sprinkle with paprika and serve at once.

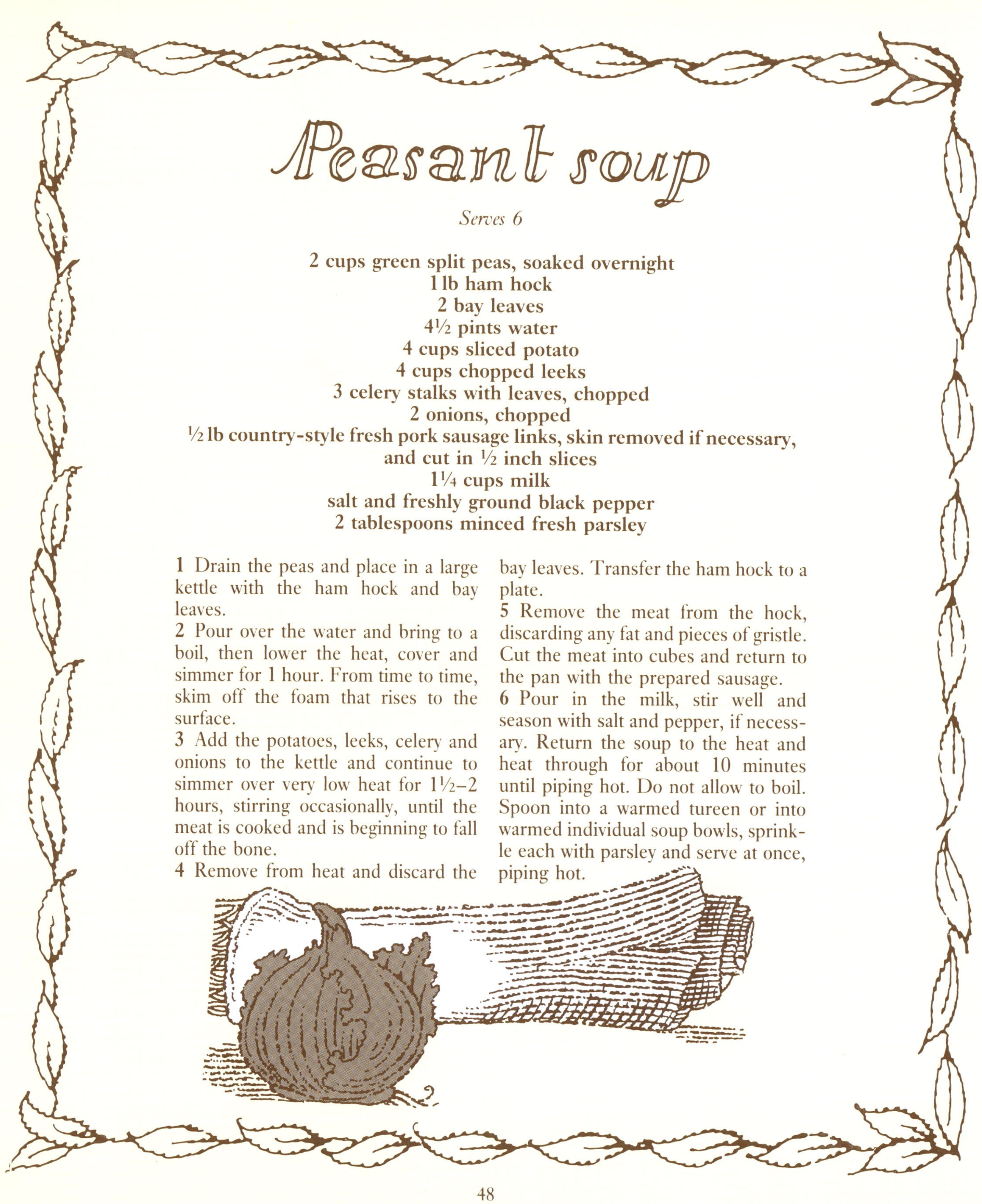

Peasant soup

Serves 6

2 cups green split peas, soaked overnight
1 lb ham hock
2 bay leaves
4½ pints water
4 cups sliced potato
4 cups chopped leeks
3 celery stalks with leaves, chopped
2 onions, chopped
½ lb country-style fresh pork sausage links, skin removed if necessary, and cut in ½ inch slices
1¼ cups milk
salt and freshly ground black pepper
2 tablespoons minced fresh parsley

1 Drain the peas and place in a large kettle with the ham hock and bay leaves.

2 Pour over the water and bring to a boil, then lower the heat, cover and simmer for 1 hour. From time to time, skim off the foam that rises to the surface.

3 Add the potatoes, leeks, celery and onions to the kettle and continue to simmer over very low heat for 1½–2 hours, stirring occasionally, until the meat is cooked and is beginning to fall off the bone.

4 Remove from heat and discard the bay leaves. Transfer the ham hock to a plate.

5 Remove the meat from the hock, discarding any fat and pieces of gristle. Cut the meat into cubes and return to the pan with the prepared sausage.

6 Pour in the milk, stir well and season with salt and pepper, if necessary. Return the soup to the heat and heat through for about 10 minutes until piping hot. Do not allow to boil. Spoon into a warmed tureen or into warmed individual soup bowls, sprinkle each with parsley and serve at once, piping hot.

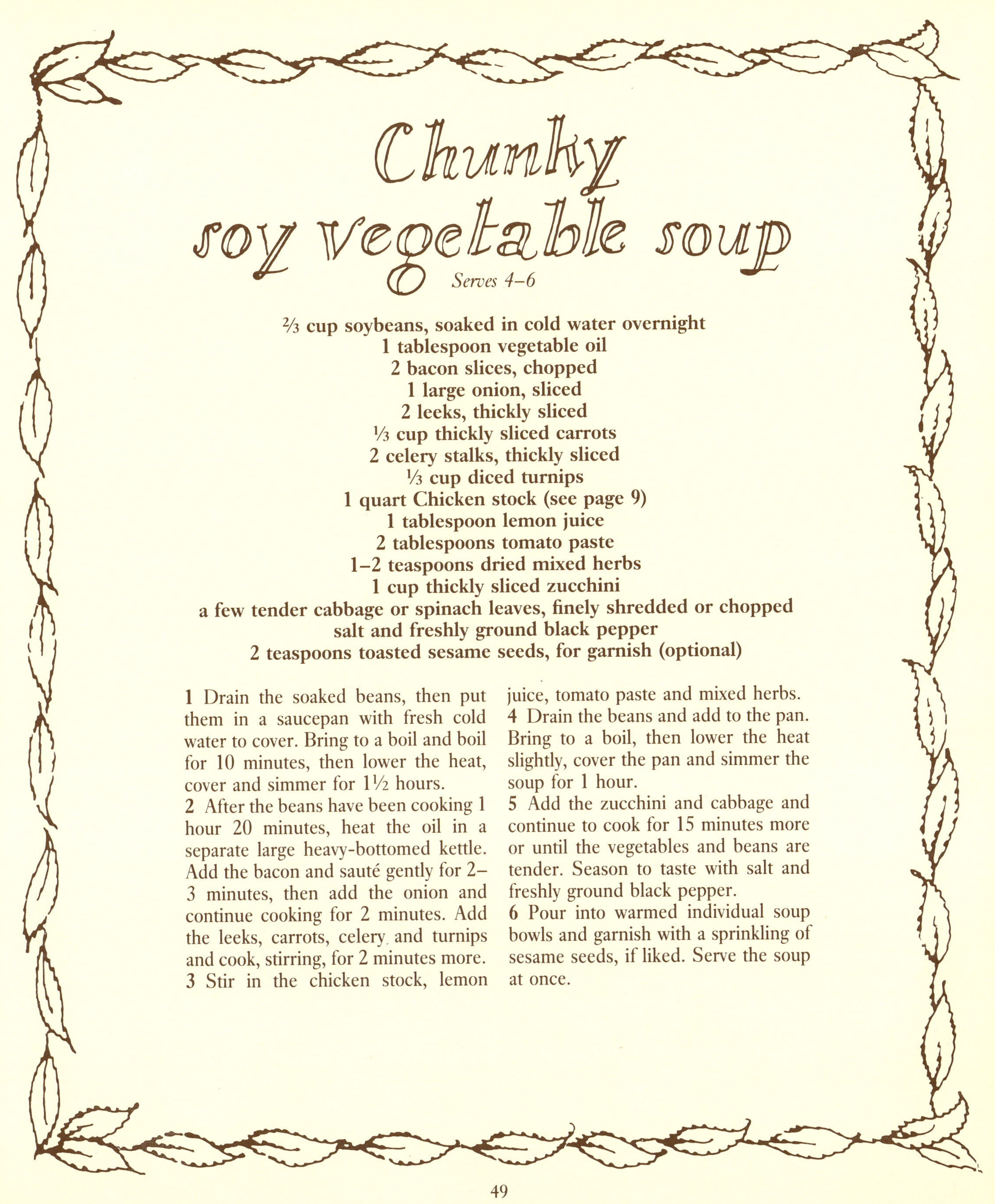

Chunky soy vegetable soup

Serves 4–6

⅔ cup soybeans, soaked in cold water overnight
1 tablespoon vegetable oil
2 bacon slices, chopped
1 large onion, sliced
2 leeks, thickly sliced
⅓ cup thickly sliced carrots
2 celery stalks, thickly sliced
⅓ cup diced turnips
1 quart Chicken stock (see page 9)
1 tablespoon lemon juice
2 tablespoons tomato paste
1–2 teaspoons dried mixed herbs
1 cup thickly sliced zucchini
a few tender cabbage or spinach leaves, finely shredded or chopped
salt and freshly ground black pepper
2 teaspoons toasted sesame seeds, for garnish (optional)

1 Drain the soaked beans, then put them in a saucepan with fresh cold water to cover. Bring to a boil and boil for 10 minutes, then lower the heat, cover and simmer for 1½ hours.

2 After the beans have been cooking 1 hour 20 minutes, heat the oil in a separate large heavy-bottomed kettle. Add the bacon and sauté gently for 2–3 minutes, then add the onion and continue cooking for 2 minutes. Add the leeks, carrots, celery and turnips and cook, stirring, for 2 minutes more.

3 Stir in the chicken stock, lemon juice, tomato paste and mixed herbs.

4 Drain the beans and add to the pan. Bring to a boil, then lower the heat slightly, cover the pan and simmer the soup for 1 hour.

5 Add the zucchini and cabbage and continue to cook for 15 minutes more or until the vegetables and beans are tender. Season to taste with salt and freshly ground black pepper.

6 Pour into warmed individual soup bowls and garnish with a sprinkling of sesame seeds, if liked. Serve the soup at once.

Chilled Soups

When the temperature soars, it's time to take a new look at soups. Forget the steaming, brimming bowls that are so sustaining in the winter and treat your friends or family to these cool creations instead. Here you will find a clear consommé, full of the goodness of beef stock; a delicious shrimp soup, enriched with cream; and a wonderful, nutty walnut soup, sure to be a success when you entertain. Chilled summer soups are a variation on the salad theme too – thanks to the freshest of vegetables, straight from the country garden, you can refresh jaded taste buds with Lettuce cooler, Iced zucchini & cheese soup or Yogurt salad soup. This selection of cold soups is sure to add a touch of luxury to any meal.

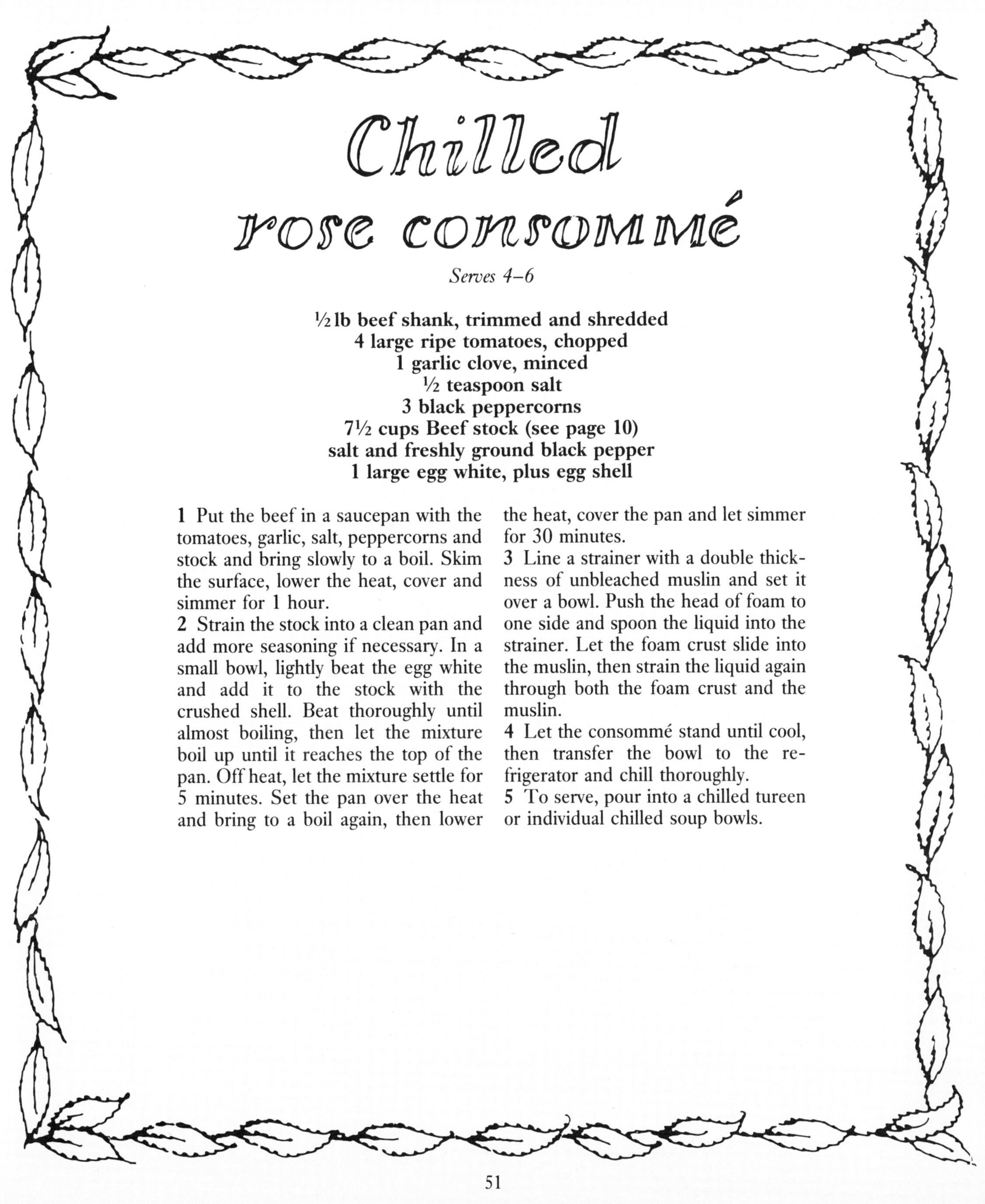

Chilled rose consommé

Serves 4–6

½ lb beef shank, trimmed and shredded
4 large ripe tomatoes, chopped
1 garlic clove, minced
½ teaspoon salt
3 black peppercorns
7½ cups Beef stock (see page 10)
salt and freshly ground black pepper
1 large egg white, plus egg shell

1 Put the beef in a saucepan with the tomatoes, garlic, salt, peppercorns and stock and bring slowly to a boil. Skim the surface, lower the heat, cover and simmer for 1 hour.

2 Strain the stock into a clean pan and add more seasoning if necessary. In a small bowl, lightly beat the egg white and add it to the stock with the crushed shell. Beat thoroughly until almost boiling, then let the mixture boil up until it reaches the top of the pan. Off heat, let the mixture settle for 5 minutes. Set the pan over the heat and bring to a boil again, then lower the heat, cover the pan and let simmer for 30 minutes.

3 Line a strainer with a double thickness of unbleached muslin and set it over a bowl. Push the head of foam to one side and spoon the liquid into the strainer. Let the foam crust slide into the muslin, then strain the liquid again through both the foam crust and the muslin.

4 Let the consommé stand until cool, then transfer the bowl to the refrigerator and chill thoroughly.

5 To serve, pour into a chilled tureen or individual chilled soup bowls.

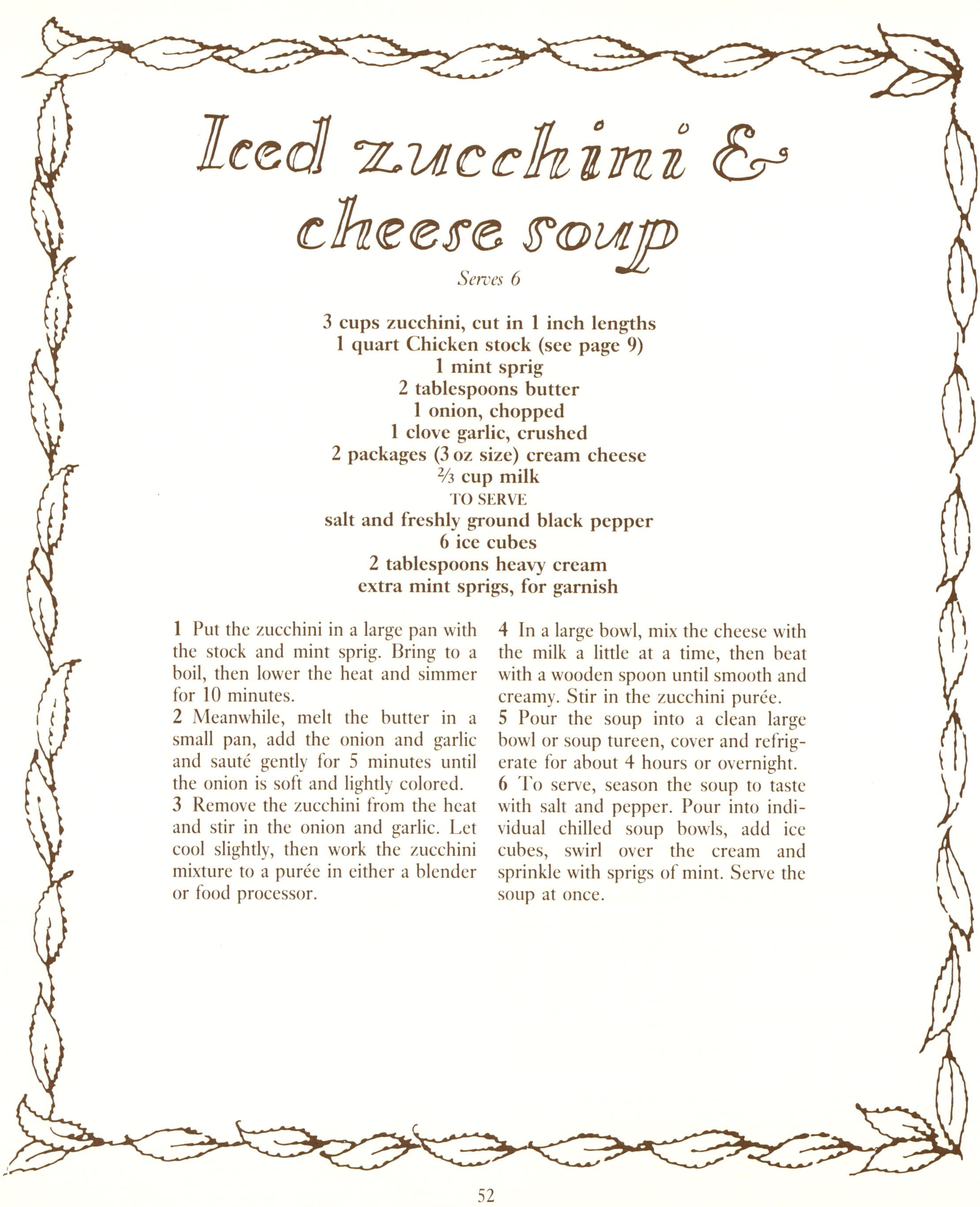

Iced zucchini & cheese soup

Serves 6

3 cups zucchini, cut in 1 inch lengths
1 quart Chicken stock (see page 9)
1 mint sprig
2 tablespoons butter
1 onion, chopped
1 clove garlic, crushed
2 packages (3 oz size) cream cheese
⅔ cup milk
TO SERVE
salt and freshly ground black pepper
6 ice cubes
2 tablespoons heavy cream
extra mint sprigs, for garnish

1 Put the zucchini in a large pan with the stock and mint sprig. Bring to a boil, then lower the heat and simmer for 10 minutes.

2 Meanwhile, melt the butter in a small pan, add the onion and garlic and sauté gently for 5 minutes until the onion is soft and lightly colored.

3 Remove the zucchini from the heat and stir in the onion and garlic. Let cool slightly, then work the zucchini mixture to a purée in either a blender or food processor.

4 In a large bowl, mix the cheese with the milk a little at a time, then beat with a wooden spoon until smooth and creamy. Stir in the zucchini purée.

5 Pour the soup into a clean large bowl or soup tureen, cover and refrigerate for about 4 hours or overnight.

6 To serve, season the soup to taste with salt and pepper. Pour into individual chilled soup bowls, add ice cubes, swirl over the cream and sprinkle with sprigs of mint. Serve the soup at once.

Yogurt salad soup

Serves 4–6

2½ cups plain yogurt, chilled
2½ cups tomato juice, chilled
1 teaspoon tomato paste
½ small cucumber, pared and finely diced
1 green pepper, seeded and finely chopped
2 scallions, thinly sliced
juice and grated rind of 1 large lemon
salt and freshly ground black pepper
large pinch of cayenne
½ teaspoon mild paprika
1 tablespoon chopped chives
thin lemon slices, for garnish
lemon wedges, to serve

1 Tip the yogurt into a large bowl and gradually beat in the tomato juice and paste until the mixture is smooth and well combined.

2 Stir in the cucumber, green pepper, scallions, lemon juice and rind. Season to taste with salt and black pepper and then stir in the cayenne and paprika.

3 Cover and refrigerate for at least 4 hours. Just before serving, stir in the chopped chives.

4 To serve, pour the soup into chilled soup bowls and garnish with lemon slices. Pass lemon wedges separately.

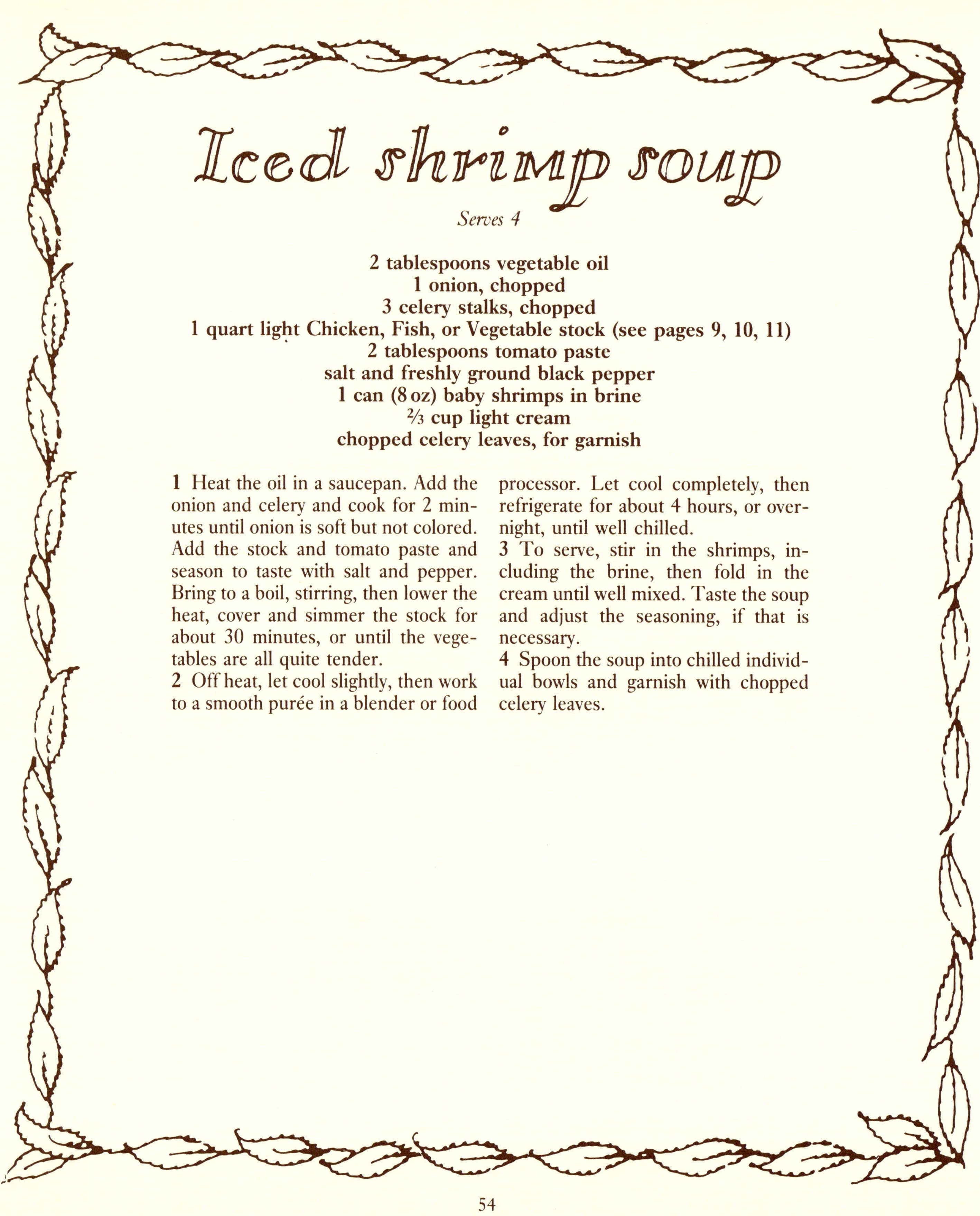

Iced shrimp soup

Serves 4

2 tablespoons vegetable oil
1 onion, chopped
3 celery stalks, chopped
1 quart light Chicken, Fish, or Vegetable stock (see pages 9, 10, 11)
2 tablespoons tomato paste
salt and freshly ground black pepper
1 can (8 oz) baby shrimps in brine
⅔ cup light cream
chopped celery leaves, for garnish

1 Heat the oil in a saucepan. Add the onion and celery and cook for 2 minutes until onion is soft but not colored. Add the stock and tomato paste and season to taste with salt and pepper. Bring to a boil, stirring, then lower the heat, cover and simmer the stock for about 30 minutes, or until the vegetables are all quite tender.

2 Off heat, let cool slightly, then work to a smooth purée in a blender or food processor. Let cool completely, then refrigerate for about 4 hours, or overnight, until well chilled.

3 To serve, stir in the shrimps, including the brine, then fold in the cream until well mixed. Taste the soup and adjust the seasoning, if that is necessary.

4 Spoon the soup into chilled individual bowls and garnish with chopped celery leaves.

Chilled asparagus soup

Serves 8

1 lb fresh asparagus, cut in 2 inch lengths
2 chicken bouillon cubes
salt and freshly ground white pepper
½ cup light cream
juice of 2 limes
FOR GARNISH
8 whole shrimp in shells (optional)
8 thin fresh slices of lime, cut through to the center
about 3 tablespoons light cream

1 Bring a large pan of cold water to a boil, add the asparagus stalks and cook for about 15 minutes until soft. Remove the asparagus with a slotted spoon and place it in the goblet of a blender or food processor.

2 Rapidly boil the liquid left in the pan for 5 minutes, then measure out 5 cups. Add the bouillon cubes to the measured liquid and stir until dissolved. Let the liquid cool slightly.

3 Add a little of the stock to the asparagus in the blender or food processor and work to a smooth purée.

4 Pour the asparagus purée into a large bowl, gradually stir in the remaining stock and season to taste with salt and pepper.

5 Stir in the cream, mixing thoroughly, then gradually add the lime juice. Cover the bowl of soup and refrigerate for 2 hours until well chilled.

6 To serve: Pour the soup into 8 chilled individual soup bowls and hook 1 shrimp, if using, and a lime slice over the side of each bowl. Swirl 1 teaspoon of cream into each bowl of soup, and then serve at once.

Blushing beet soup

Serves 8

1½ lb uncooked beet
7½ cups Chicken stock (see page 9)
1 teaspoon salt
1 tablespoon red wine vinegar
1 teaspoon sugar
1¼ cups dairy sour cream
juice of 1 small lemon
freshly ground black pepper
1 cucumber, pared and diced
6 scallions, finely sliced

1 Peel the beet, then grate roughly.
2 Put the grated beet in a large heavy-bottomed kettle with the stock, salt, vinegar and sugar. Bring to a boil, stir well, then lower the heat, half cover and simmer gently for 45 minutes.
3 Pour the soup into a bowl, cool, cover and refrigerate overnight.
4 Pass the soup through a nylon strainer into a large tureen, reserving the beet left in the strainer.
5 Stir the sour cream until smooth and free of lumps, then beat gradually into the soup. Stir in the lemon juice and season well with black pepper.
6 Stir the reserved beet into the soup together with the cucumber and two-thirds of the scallions. Cover and refrigerate until required.
7 To serve: Pour into a chilled tureen or chilled individual soup bowls and sprinkle with the remaining scallions.

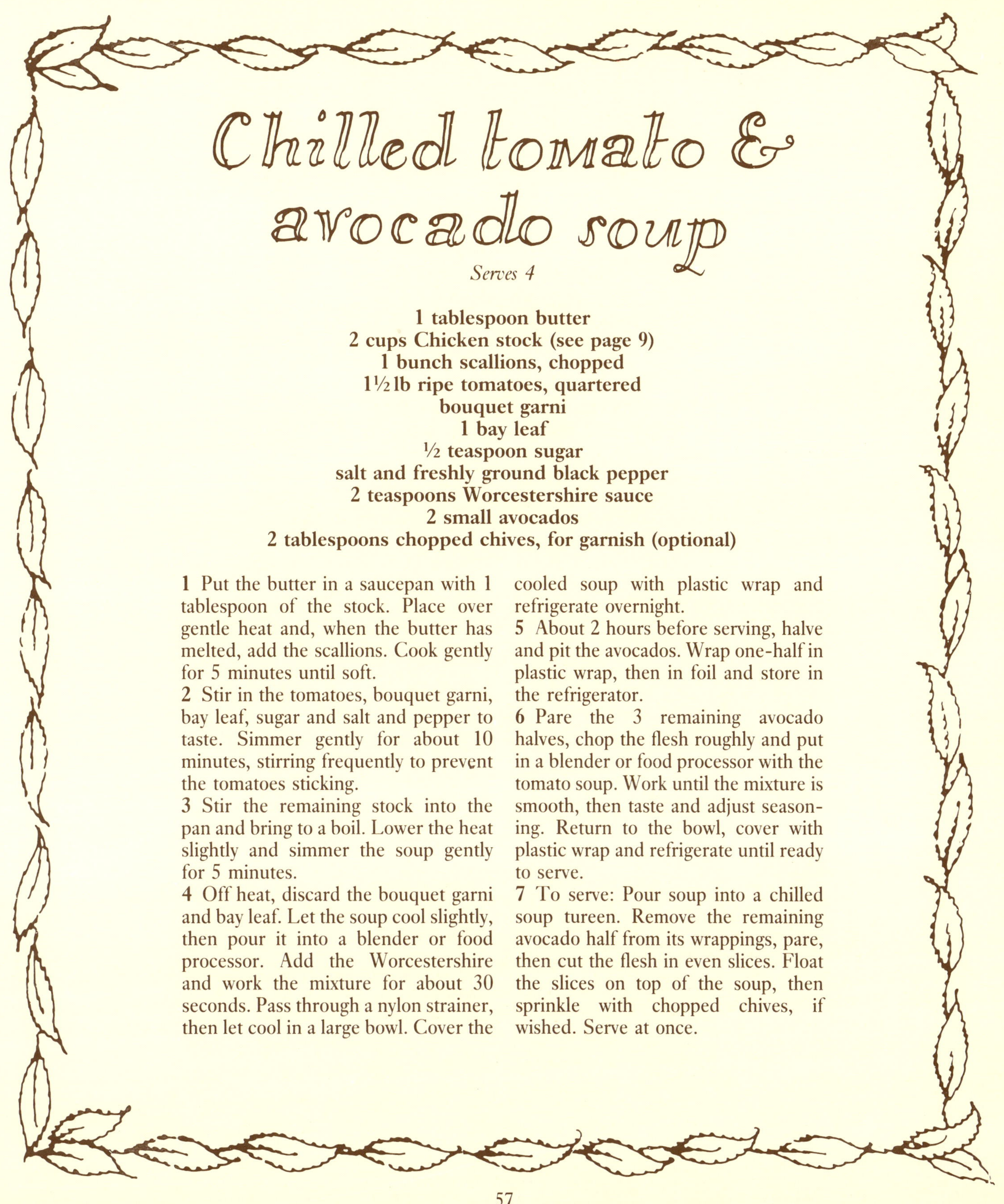

Chilled tomato & avocado soup

Serves 4

1 tablespoon butter
2 cups Chicken stock (see page 9)
1 bunch scallions, chopped
1½ lb ripe tomatoes, quartered
bouquet garni
1 bay leaf
½ teaspoon sugar
salt and freshly ground black pepper
2 teaspoons Worcestershire sauce
2 small avocados
2 tablespoons chopped chives, for garnish (optional)

1 Put the butter in a saucepan with 1 tablespoon of the stock. Place over gentle heat and, when the butter has melted, add the scallions. Cook gently for 5 minutes until soft.

2 Stir in the tomatoes, bouquet garni, bay leaf, sugar and salt and pepper to taste. Simmer gently for about 10 minutes, stirring frequently to prevent the tomatoes sticking.

3 Stir the remaining stock into the pan and bring to a boil. Lower the heat slightly and simmer the soup gently for 5 minutes.

4 Off heat, discard the bouquet garni and bay leaf. Let the soup cool slightly, then pour it into a blender or food processor. Add the Worcestershire and work the mixture for about 30 seconds. Pass through a nylon strainer, then let cool in a large bowl. Cover the cooled soup with plastic wrap and refrigerate overnight.

5 About 2 hours before serving, halve and pit the avocados. Wrap one-half in plastic wrap, then in foil and store in the refrigerator.

6 Pare the 3 remaining avocado halves, chop the flesh roughly and put in a blender or food processor with the tomato soup. Work until the mixture is smooth, then taste and adjust seasoning. Return to the bowl, cover with plastic wrap and refrigerate until ready to serve.

7 To serve: Pour soup into a chilled soup tureen. Remove the remaining avocado half from its wrappings, pare, then cut the flesh in even slices. Float the slices on top of the soup, then sprinkle with chopped chives, if wished. Serve at once.

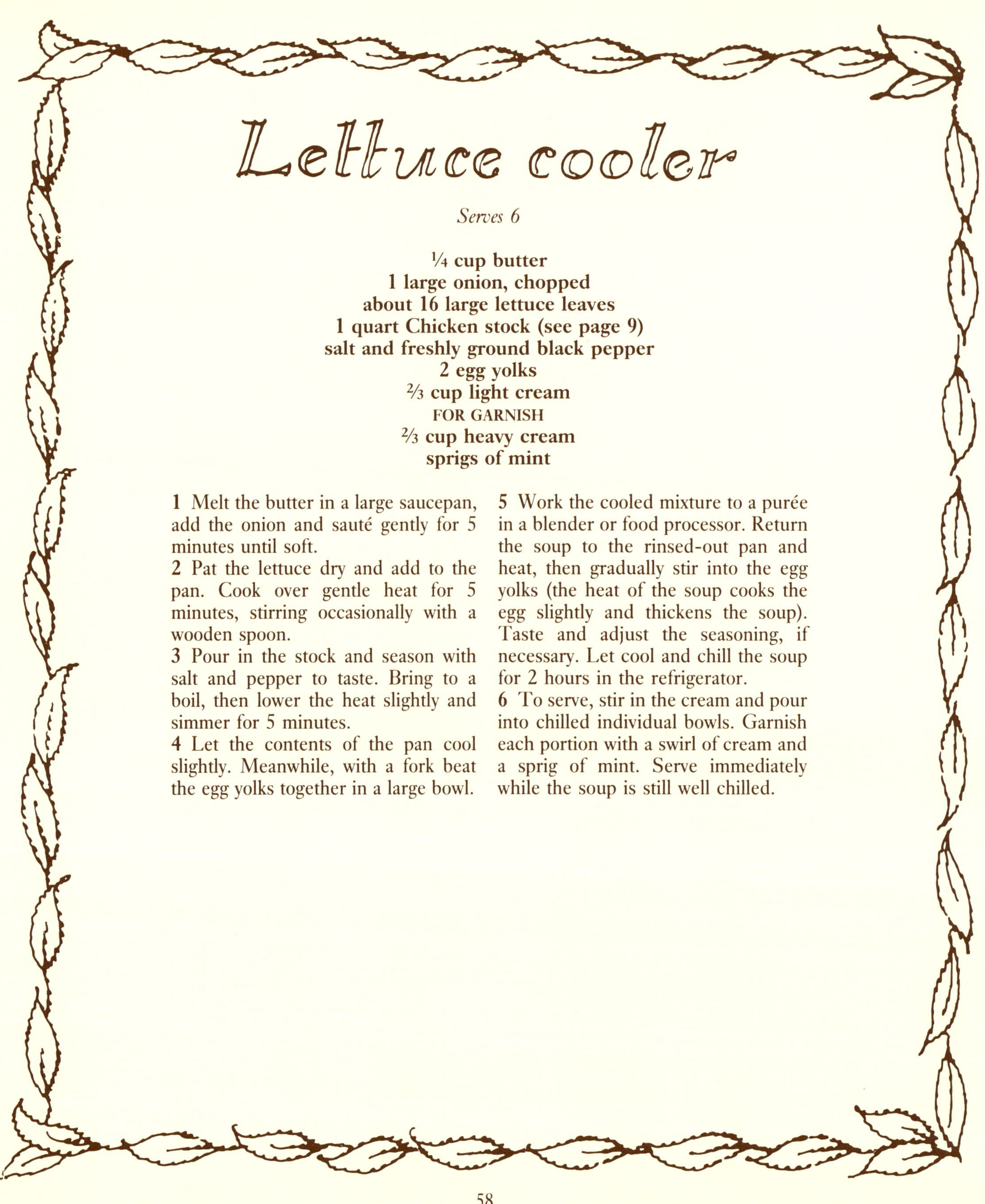

Lettuce cooler

Serves 6

¼ cup butter
1 large onion, chopped
about 16 large lettuce leaves
1 quart Chicken stock (see page 9)
salt and freshly ground black pepper
2 egg yolks
⅔ cup light cream
FOR GARNISH
⅔ cup heavy cream
sprigs of mint

1 Melt the butter in a large saucepan, add the onion and sauté gently for 5 minutes until soft.
2 Pat the lettuce dry and add to the pan. Cook over gentle heat for 5 minutes, stirring occasionally with a wooden spoon.
3 Pour in the stock and season with salt and pepper to taste. Bring to a boil, then lower the heat slightly and simmer for 5 minutes.
4 Let the contents of the pan cool slightly. Meanwhile, with a fork beat the egg yolks together in a large bowl.
5 Work the cooled mixture to a purée in a blender or food processor. Return the soup to the rinsed-out pan and heat, then gradually stir into the egg yolks (the heat of the soup cooks the egg slightly and thickens the soup). Taste and adjust the seasoning, if necessary. Let cool and chill the soup for 2 hours in the refrigerator.
6 To serve, stir in the cream and pour into chilled individual bowls. Garnish each portion with a swirl of cream and a sprig of mint. Serve immediately while the soup is still well chilled.

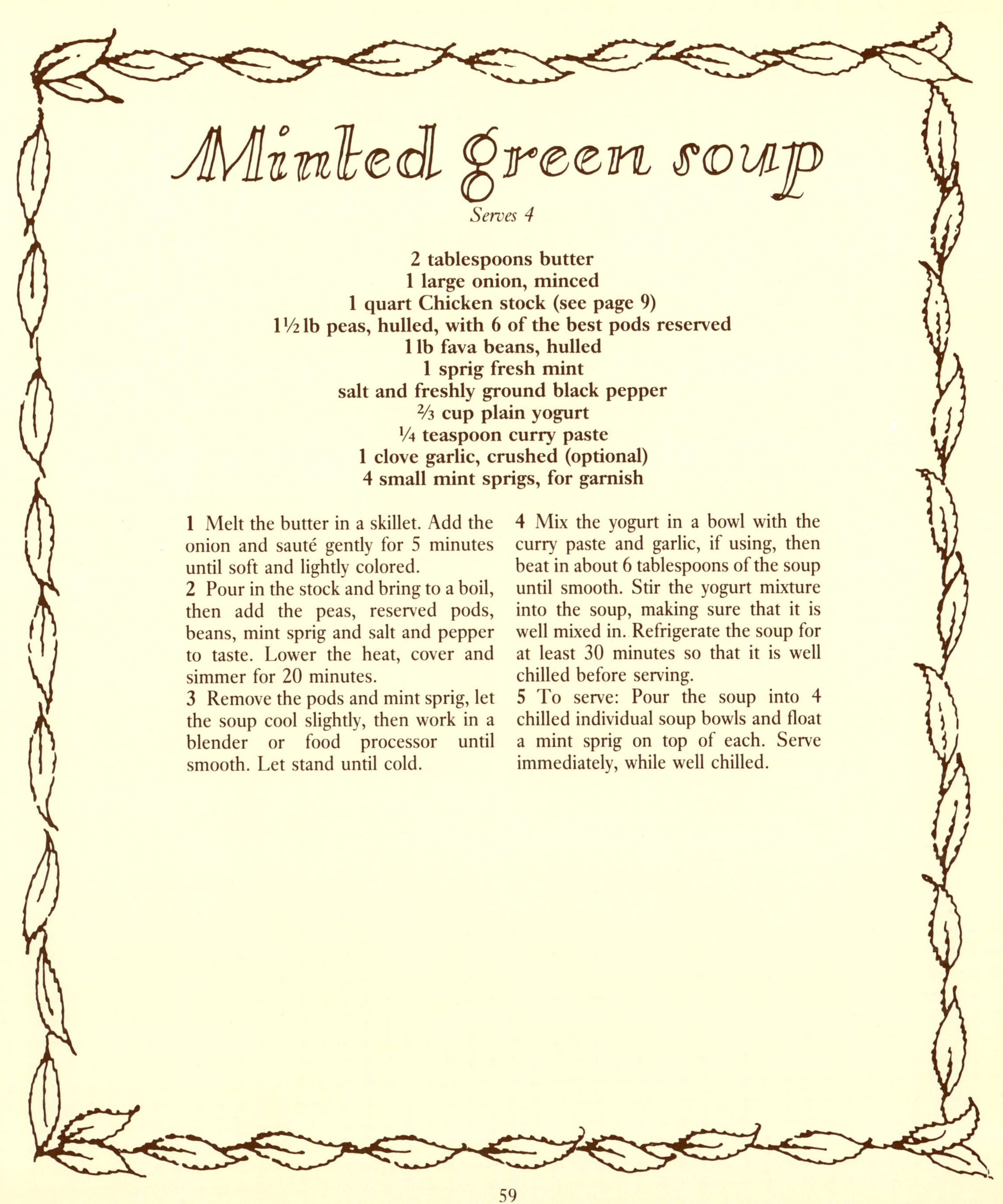

Minted green soup

Serves 4

2 tablespoons butter
1 large onion, minced
1 quart Chicken stock (see page 9)
1½ lb peas, hulled, with 6 of the best pods reserved
1 lb fava beans, hulled
1 sprig fresh mint
salt and freshly ground black pepper
⅔ cup plain yogurt
¼ teaspoon curry paste
1 clove garlic, crushed (optional)
4 small mint sprigs, for garnish

1 Melt the butter in a skillet. Add the onion and sauté gently for 5 minutes until soft and lightly colored.

2 Pour in the stock and bring to a boil, then add the peas, reserved pods, beans, mint sprig and salt and pepper to taste. Lower the heat, cover and simmer for 20 minutes.

3 Remove the pods and mint sprig, let the soup cool slightly, then work in a blender or food processor until smooth. Let stand until cold.

4 Mix the yogurt in a bowl with the curry paste and garlic, if using, then beat in about 6 tablespoons of the soup until smooth. Stir the yogurt mixture into the soup, making sure that it is well mixed in. Refrigerate the soup for at least 30 minutes so that it is well chilled before serving.

5 To serve: Pour the soup into 4 chilled individual soup bowls and float a mint sprig on top of each. Serve immediately, while well chilled.

Chilled sweet 'n' sour soup

Serves 6

4 tablespoons golden raisins
4 cups plain yogurt, chilled
⅔ cup dairy sour cream, chilled
⅔ cup ice water
salt and freshly ground black pepper
1 medium-size cucumber, shredded
4–5 scallions, chopped
6 ice cubes
3–4 sprigs fresh mint

1 Put the golden raisins in a small bowl with water to cover and set them aside for 30 minutes.

2 Meanwhile, in a large bowl, beat the yogurt, sour cream and ice water together until smooth. Add salt and pepper to taste. Stir in the cucumber and scallions. Cover the bowl and put it in the refrigerator for at least 4 hours, or until well chilled.

3 Just before serving, drain the raisins. Divide the soup among 6 chilled individual soup bowls, add an ice cube to each bowl and sprinkle each portion with sprigs of fresh mint and the golden raisins.

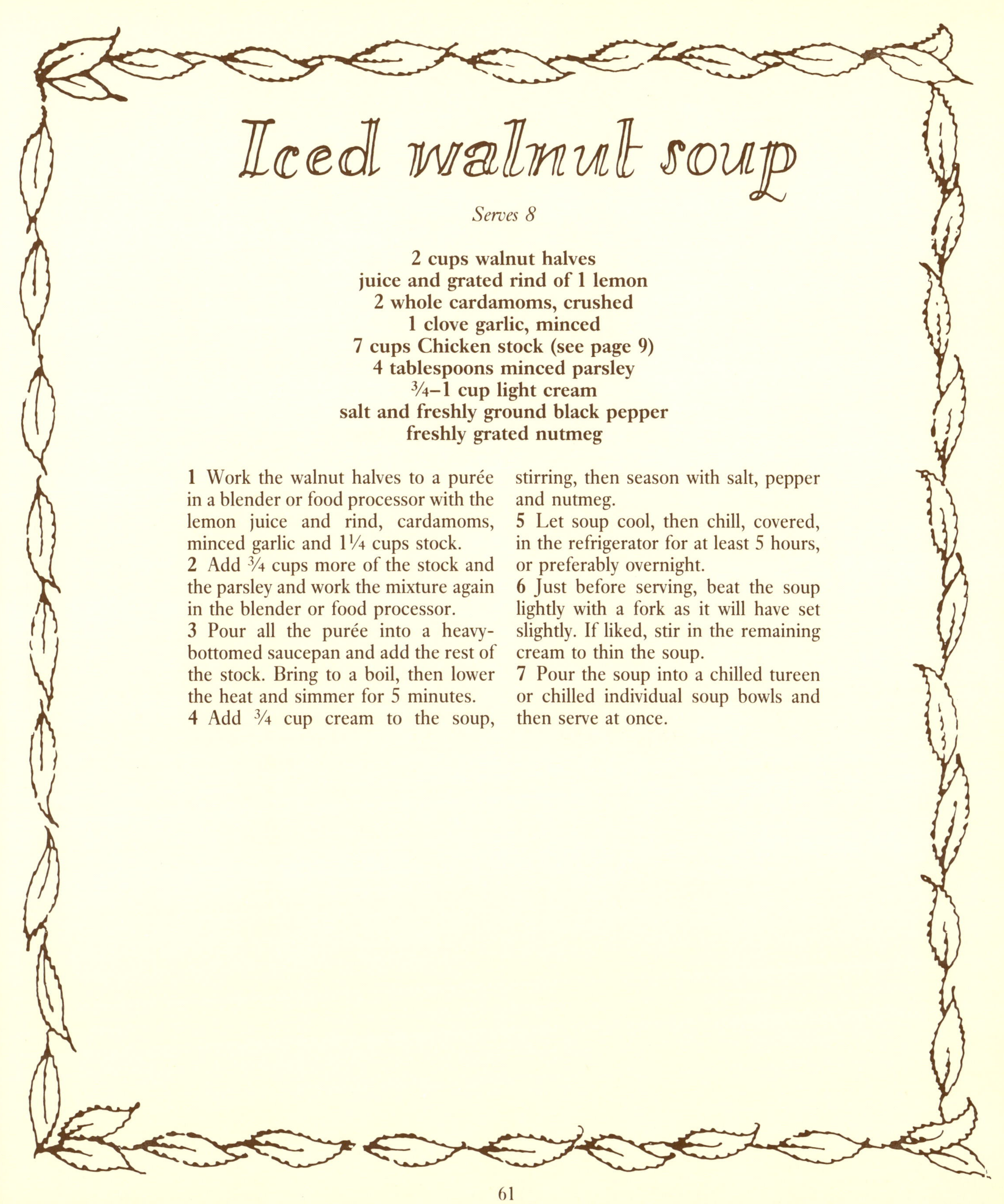

Iced walnut soup

Serves 8

2 cups walnut halves
juice and grated rind of 1 lemon
2 whole cardamoms, crushed
1 clove garlic, minced
7 cups Chicken stock (see page 9)
4 tablespoons minced parsley
¾–1 cup light cream
salt and freshly ground black pepper
freshly grated nutmeg

1 Work the walnut halves to a purée in a blender or food processor with the lemon juice and rind, cardamoms, minced garlic and 1¼ cups stock.

2 Add ¾ cups more of the stock and the parsley and work the mixture again in the blender or food processor.

3 Pour all the purée into a heavy-bottomed saucepan and add the rest of the stock. Bring to a boil, then lower the heat and simmer for 5 minutes.

4 Add ¾ cup cream to the soup, stirring, then season with salt, pepper and nutmeg.

5 Let soup cool, then chill, covered, in the refrigerator for at least 5 hours, or preferably overnight.

6 Just before serving, beat the soup lightly with a fork as it will have set slightly. If liked, stir in the remaining cream to thin the soup.

7 Pour the soup into a chilled tureen or chilled individual soup bowls and then serve at once.

Orange & carrot smoothie

Serves 4

1 tablespoon vegetable oil
1 onion, minced
2 tablespoons medium-dry sherry (optional)
3 cups thinly sliced carrots
2½ cups Chicken stock (see page 9)
salt and freshly ground black pepper
grated rind of 1 orange
juice of 3 large oranges
1 small carrot, shredded, for garnish

1 Heat the oil in a saucepan, add the onion and sauté gently for 5 minutes until soft and lightly colored. Add the sherry, if using, and bring to a boil.

2 Add the sliced carrots and stock to the pan and add salt and freshly ground black pepper to taste.

3 Bring to a boil, stirring, then lower the heat, cover and simmer gently for 45 minutes until the carrots are very tender. Let cool.

4 Work the soup to a purée in a blender or food processor. Pour the purée into a bowl, cover and refrigerate the soup for at least 2 hours or preferably overnight.

5 Just before serving, stir the orange rind and juice into the soup, then taste and adjust seasoning. Pour into 4 chilled individual soup bowls, sprinkle a little shredded carrot over each bowl and serve at once.

Crimson fruit soup

Serves 4

3/4 pint fresh or frozen red currants
3/4 pint fresh or frozen black currants
3/4 pint fresh or frozen raspberries
1 quart water
3 tablespoons quick-cooking tapioca
2 inch cinnamon stick
2 thinly pared strips lemon rind
1 cup superfine sugar
1/3 cup dairy sour cream, beaten until smooth

1 Prepare all the fruit, if using fresh. Reserve 4 raspberries for the garnish.
2 Put the fruits in a large kettle with the water, tapioca, cinnamon stick, lemon rind and sugar.
3 Set over medium heat and bring to a boil, stirring. Lower the heat and simmer, uncovered, for 10 minutes.
4 Off heat, discard the cinnamon stick and lemon rind. Pass the soup through a strainer. Cool, then refrigerate for 1½ hours.
5 Pour the soup into 4 chilled individual bowls. Swirl a portion of sour cream over each serving. Top each swirl with a raspberry. Serve at once.

Black cherry soup

Serves 4–6

2 lb fresh Bing cherries
7 oz sugar
pinch of ground cinnamon
1 cup water
1½ teaspoons potato flour

1 Pit the cherries and put them in a large saucepan with the sugar, cinnamon and 7/8 cup water. Cook the cherries over low heat until they are soft.
2 Mix the potato flour with the remaining water and add it to the cherries. Continue cooking the soup gently until it thickens a little, then remove it from the heat.
3 Cool the soup to room temperature and serve, or chill it in the refrigerator before serving.

Index